THE
CRAIG BROWN
OMNIBUS

For Willie Donaldson

Published in Great Britain by
Private Eye Productions Ltd, 6 Carlisle Street, W1V 5RG.
© 1999 Pressdram Ltd
ISBN 1 901784 169
Designed by Bridget Tisdall
Printed in England by Ebenezer Baylis & Son Ltd, Worcester
2 4 6 8 10 9 7 5 3 1

THE
CRAIG BROWN
OMNIBUS

THE DIARIES FROM
PRIVATE EYE
1995-1999

PRIVATE EYE

FOREWORD

BY EDWARD WINDSOR &
SOPHIE WESSEX

EDWARD: Tremendous! We'— that's to say, my wife and I — share a tremendous —

SOPHIE: — sense of humour. In fact one of the things that initially attracted me to the challenge of annexing with what, for the sake of convenience, one might term the whole "Royal Family product" was that Edward laughed at the same things I laughed at — and at more or less the same time. On top of this, I felt any future partnership could benefit from my skills and experience in increasing brand awareness. It's our aim to upturn perception of our jointly-owned sense of humour, so it's excellent to have been invited to involve ourselves in this introductory pitch.

EDWARD: Tremendous! Actually, there's a tremendously amusing anecdote about —

SOPHIE: Because let's face it, I don't want to be branded as "A Royal Wife". As I see it, my market niche should appeal to a wider public across a broad-based social spectrum, and this target will be facilitated through the free-flow of access to our joint sense of humour. So let's keep it brief and say that this book-style project is a —

EDWARD: — "tremendously enjoyable"?

SOPHIE: an accessible and well-focused addition to the highly competitive niche of middle-market humour.

EDWARD: And a literally tremendous —

SOPHIE: That's all we've got time for. Ciao!

MAYA ANGELOU

Heed well the wisdom of our ancestors, my sons and daughters, for it is rough-hewn by time. "The birdy does not sit on the tree; it is the tree that sits on the birdy." The wise man will recognise this as correct in all its essentials. And another old African saying also proves as true today as it ever was: "He travels furthest who never leaves his homestead." For the human heart is a rock containing much water and bundles of sweet fruits; a rock that can soar in the air, flying higher than the steepest lakes. And before it comes to rest, this rock will gallop as fast as a speckled hen, eager to rest its head on the distant murmur of soft glades. So heed ye well the wisdom of our ancestors. And learn.

❖

Let us listen awhile, for those without ears shall never hear. When I was but a little bitty girl, I would sit at the feet

5

of my Grandmother, ready for my lessons.

"Tell me 'bout the time you wuz a little girl, Granmaw" I'd beg her. And as she opened her mouth, I'd remind her that I was now a little girl, just as she'd once been.

"That's true, honey," she'd say, "And when I was 'bout your age, I —"

"And you know what I've learnt from being a little girl, Granmawmaw?" I would interject.

"Why, no, honey, I don't, but when ah was jist 'bout your age I —"

"I've learned, Granmawmaw, that to be seven years of age on this extraordinary planet of ours, with its mountains and its valleys, its deserts and its lakes, its skyscrapers and its bungalows, its wealthy and its downtrodden, its honey-bees buzzing on scented lilac in the warmth of the summer breeze, its lovers whispering sweet nothings to each other amidst the ceaseless clamour of the city turmoil, its soaring beauty — as beautiful a beauty as ever beauteous beauty was beautiful — and its grinding poverty, particularly among the poor — why, Granmawmaw, I've learned that to be seven years of age on this extraordinary planet is —"

But at this point, I would glance over at my Grandmother, and I would notice that her eyes were firmly closed, with cacophonous snores emerging like paddle steamers on the old Mississippi from her mouth.

"Wake up, Granmawmaw!" I would thereby exclaim. But, in the soundness of her sleep she would remain deaf to my lessons.

Sad to relate, my grandmother died without ever learning anything from the little girl who would one day grow up to be Dr Maya Angelou, professor, poet, Grammy-winner, Emmy-winner, Laureate to the nation. Truly, those without ears will never hear.

❖

There is an old African saying, never truer today than yesterday or the day before: "The stony path is best travelled with bare feet." Africa — my Africa — is rich in such wisdom. It is the heartland of beauty, the boiling-pot of spirituality, the very crucible of all art and literature. Believe me, there is no great writer or painter who is not at heart an African. "To be or not to be" — the rich reggae rhythm is undeniable. The culture of Africa — simple, heartfelt, full of grace and hope — is everything that America is not. And that is why I chose for my present homestead a dwelling in North Carolina with the deepest, bluest, longest, widest, most heatingdest swimming pool you ever did see. For only by sitting in a beautiful sun-lounger, as black as my people but with an orange trim, surrounding myself with such bluey warmth, such warm blueyness, such bluthy warmeyness, can I feel truly back among my people in Africa, bathing in their grace, their simplicity, their great freedom from earthly possessions.

❖

Mine was the privilege that momentous day in our nation's history to orate a poem at the inauguration of President Bill Clinton, a poem both as forceful and full of force as the strongest breeze. And I recite it again today, six long, short, long years later, rewritten and reworked to make it fly with the wings of a gazelle across the stage of our times:

Lift up your face, America, you have a piercing need
To breathe awhile as your President signs
A hefty wad of worthy documentation
Entrusted to his doughty hand by a nation
Kneeling before him in gratitude.
At last he has done with his signing; open wide your lips,
To accommodate the hard-pressed vessel
Heading fast towards its port in these storm-tossed times.

For his bright new morning glory is dawning just for you
And, if faced with courage, its passion spent, need not be
Faced again until the dawn. After which
His lawyers will deny every charge you care to make, you
                                                    dumb-ass ho.

Good Morning America!

❖

Oprah Winfrey. Just two short words, one of five letters, the other of seven letters. But with a meaning deeper than the deepest glacier, a reverberation lower than the highest bridge. In Africa, there is an old saying, passed down to us from village ancestors long gone. "On a rainy afternoon, the talk-show host doth occupy the time of the bored." Never have these true words been truer of anyone than of Oprah. Why, even the letters of her Christian name spell "A Hoper", leastways once you've re-shuffled them and added an "e" just before the final "r".

Oprah goes where the fearful will not tread. Her eyes fill with salty tears — tears rough-hewn from strong onions cultivated in the deepest earth of her own dreams — as she listens with ears athwart to what the poor and the downtrodden have to tell us. After they have finished telling their tales, Oprah looks with downcast eyes towards we, her viewers. "Don't go away," she says, caringly, "We'll be back after this short break."

One day, we, the African-Americans, will all have our own talk-shows, we will all listen while others weep and groan, we will all rise up those studio staircases, our microphones firmly in our hands. But until that day comes we would do well to view Oprah, all day, every day, and to respect that old saying from my African homeland: "The man who wears his shoe on his ear will remain deaf to the sound of his feet." Bless you, my children.

LORD ARCHER'S
CAMPAIGN DIARY

I stood with John Major in his garden at Huntingdon on the morning of the General Election. It was a worrying time for the 3 of us — but he had come to value my company for 6 things:

My transparent integrity.

My political nous.

My ability to communicate.

And my way with words.

Yes, I wasn't afraid to tell it to him like what it was — and, like Margaret Thatcher, President J.F. Kennedy and Nelson Mandela before him, he respected me for it.

"What's going to happen, Jeffrey?" said the Prime Minister, through misty eyes, his voice trembling.

I looked the guy straight in the eye. I was good at looking people straight in the eye. I gained a blue at it when I was a scholarship student at Harvard University — the youngest ever.

He expected the truth — and I was the man to give it to him.

"You've got to face up to it, Prime Minister. You're gonna win. That much is clear. But it might be by a slightly reduced margin."

He looked me straight in the eye.

"Jeffrey," he said, "When the time comes, I want you to take over from me as Prime Minister. You've got a lot to offer this country of ours — and, by God, Jeffrey, *we need you.*

❖

This was virtually word-for-word what the great Winston Churchill had told me when I had the immense privilege of meeting him in 1965.

The great man had taken me on as his Political Advisor after I had served a brief but record-breaking spell as the youngest-ever Professor of Economics at the LSE.

And when Winston told me this back then in 1956, I replied as I did to John Major.

"My one ambition in life," I said, "is to serve the people of London as their mayor. I can bring to the task 7 important qualities: energy, determination — and dedication.

"I have already proved myself as the youngest-ever yachtsman to sail single-handedly across America.

"I stand before you today as the British and World Chess Champion, the BBC Sports Personality of the Year, and the proud winner of the Prix Goncourt.

"But I would sacrifice each and every one of these honours if it meant I could serve the ordinary, decent people of Greater London. Pass me that baton, sir — and I will run away with it."

Winston died in my arms later that day — but I shall never forget his parting words.

He looked me straight in the eye and said, "Jeffrey — the ordinary, decent people of London deserve a Mayor like you. It is my dying wish, Jeffrey, that you become Mayor in the year 2000."

And with that Winston passed away — but not before he had given me a useful tip to invest in Anglia TV shares.

Little did the chattering classes realise when they criticised me for buying those shares that the person they were really criticising was the late, great Winston Churchill.

❖

So when I ask to be considered for election as the Mayor of London, it is with the backing not only of John and Winston — but also of my close friend His Holiness Pope John Paul II, under whom I was once privileged to serve as the youngest-ever Cardinal.

In recent months, many of my close friends have come to me and said, "Why bother, Jeffrey, you will only receive endless criticism from the chattering classes who will go to any extreme to stop you gaining the final prize."

I have looked them straight in the eye. "I have received over 2 million letters from the ordinary, decent people of London imploring me to stand," I have replied in all humility, "And in the same time I have raised over £350,000,000 for charitable causes.

"I would not be being true to my background as one of the nation's premier aristocrats (my great-grandfather was the Duke Ellington) if I were to succumb to the knockers and ignore these 3 million letters. It's not for nothing that I am the proud holder of three Lonsdale Belts, you know!"

❖

What can I deliver to the people of London? £2,000 in a plain brown envelope, yes — but that's not all. With my 90-

strong research team, I have uncovered major solutions to the serious problems faced by London.

After spending 3 months with my close friend Mayor Giuliani of New York, I have discovered that London faces crime and social problems.

After 6 months with my close friend, name forgotten add in asap, the Mayor of Athens, I have discovered that London faces problems in education and transport.

I have immediately set my 300-strong team of researchers onto the job. And these are our clear-cut and far-sighted solutions — tested and approved by up to 2000 world experts.

Transport — More vehicles on the roads equals more traffic. It's as simple as that.

Education — Our children will only learn more when they are taught more. It's as simple as that.

Crime — The only way to cut back on crime is to take steps to reduce it. It's as simple as that.

Social problems — Poverty is not caused by money — it's caused by lack of money. It's as simple as that.

❖

Having been Lord Mayor of London some time in the early 1970s — and one of the most successful ever in the post, I will have you know — or so my close friend Boris Yeltsin tells me! — I know that, with the help of my 2,000-strong research team, I have the sheer experience to roll up my sleeves and tackle the job once more.

It'll be tough, yes — but no tougher than my (admittedly modest) achievements in becoming the first-ever Briton to climb Mount Everest and winning the Pulitzer Prize three years running!

Vote Archer for Mayor — and stand a chance of winning up to £5,000,000 in my £2,000,000 prize draw!

David Bailey's
World of Fashion

David Bailey: Karl, what do you look for in a model?

Karl Lagerfeld: I look for someone who can walk. They have to be able to walk. I insist on it for all my shows. You have a model who cannot walk and what happens? She just stands and stands and stands. Eventually, we have to move her off, maybe with a fork-lift. So I never use her again. But Linda Evangelista I love. No one can walk like Linda Evangelista. She walks perfect.

Bailey: How does she walk, Karl?

Lagerfeld: First one leg, then the other, then the first one again. And so on, until she gets to where I want her to go. Then she stops. Then she repeats process, but in reverse.

Bailey: Do supermodels have to be intelligent?

Lagerfeld: Highly intelligent. To be photographed, you have to know at all times where your eyes are, where your nose is, where your hair is. You have to know everything. Jerry Hall, she is highly intelligent. She knows where her eyes are, but she also knows where her legs are. She can move her eyes and her legs at the same time. This is sophisticated. And a model must develop a rapport with the photographer. Without rapport, there is nothing. Only a photograph.

❖

David Bailey: You got a nice pair legs there, love.

Kate Moss: Bailey!

Bailey: Seersly. An I'm an expert, love, no kiddin. So, Kate, wossa worst thing's ever happened to you?

Kate: It totally did my head in. I was, like, "Hey, this has totally did my head in, kind of thing." It was like a totally did-your-head-in kind of experience. Talk about doin' your head in!

Bailey: So whappened, love?

Kate: I was, like, "I want a cuppa tea, yeah? And I poured the water in, right?" Then I was like, "Hey, this tea tastes kinda watery, right?" Then I looked into the cup, and like I'd forgotten to put the tea-bag in, yeah? It was the forgotten-to-put-the-tea-bag-in-the-cup-thing. I'd heard of it happening to other people but I never thought it'd happen to me. Really did my head in.

❖

David Bailey: Vivienne, who do you have in mind when you design?

Vivienne Westwood: For my new collection, Ludwig Wittgenstein. All layers and layers of tulle with gorgeous low-slung bodices with brocade all over, just like his philosophy. I think therefore I am. Or is it I am not? I must look it up. Depends on your mood, I suppose. You don't pronounce the "W", you know. It's really Vittgenstein. And I've been heavily influenced by that, too. My new collection comes out under the name Wivienne Vestwood.

❖

David Bailey: You're a beautiful bird, no mistake. With legs like that, you could've been a model, love. Tell me all about yourself, darlin'.

Penelope Tree: My name's Penelope. I was a model. In fact, I was married to you for five years.

David Bailey: Blimey! Strike me down with a feather! Small world!

❖

David Bailey: Naomi, you're gorgeous. You ever been late for an assignment?

Naomi Campbell: Me? As a black woman, I always arrive early. If I say I'll be there at 10am on Wednesday, I'll be there at 9.45am on Thursday, no worries.

Bailey: Do you ever get bitchy with other models, love?

Naomi: As a black woman, I've never been bitchy. I try to help others. If I'm wearing a dress they want to wear, and they've got a dress I want to wear I'll always try and switch with them. Particularly if they're shit.

Bailey: What about Nelson Mandela?

Naomi: He's not bitchy. He doesn't slag you off like some of the others, no way. Like, before I went on stage with him, he didn't start pinching me or saying catty things or trying to ladder my tights with his nails. No way. The guy's like a saint. And I treated him with respect. I've been very influenced by him. He's like the greatest supermodel of them all, and I respect that.

Bailey: Why are you so special? Because you are, and I'm an expert.

Naomi: I try to be honest with myself. When I look in the mirror, I say, "Naomi, you're beautiful, you're intelligent, you're punctual, you're generous, you're popular and you don't take no shit from anyone so those other fuckers can go fuck themselves." You really have to be honest with yourself in this business, David.

❖

David Bailey: Thierry Mugler, you're one of the all-time great designers. How important is the model when it comes to showing your clothes?

Thierry Mugler: Very important. Like yesterday, I had this truly beautiful long pink dress, but it was too full in the bust for Kate, so I pin it back. But it still not look too good, so I take out my scissors and transform it into a long skirt. All very nice, but Kate is just a bit too short, so we turn it into a mini-skirt. This would be fine — beautiful, gorgeous — but Kate is so unhappy with that length, and the model she must be happy, so I take out my scissors. Voila! We have the most amazing fantastic thin pink belt, so neat, so sexy, so feminine!

❖

David Bailey: Anna, you're now the editor of American *Vogue*. Who was your major influence?

Anna Wintour: Diana Vreeland. She was so uncompromising. Just before she died, she went overboard for yellow. Everything had to be yellow. Yellow cushions, yellow sofas, yellow tables, yellow dresses, yellow hats, walls all yellow, paintings all yellow, books all yellow, carpets all yellow. In the end, she died of jaundice. They didn't find her body for three weeks.

STEPHEN BAYLEY

Since I am widely regarded as the greatest know-all in this oh-so-cluttered metropolis, I have grown used to lesser minds calling to say, for example, "Stephen, dearest, we need to pick your massive brain! Can you tell us 10 interesting things about milk?"

Within seconds, I have nipped to the file in my brain marked "milk" and pulled out the folder headed "interesting". I then articulate with unerring clarity, elegance and thingy-wingy all I know that is interesting about milk. "It is white, exquisitely white," I say. "One can drink it, if forced to, and it comes from cows." I then pause to let them catch up with their note-taking before reopening the floodgates of fact. "It emerges from bottles or cartons, C2s devote their mornings to pouring it over breakfast flakes and the udder of a cow is a monstrous vulgarity, inelegant and implausible, one of nature's most conspicuous failures of design."

Small wonder I am so often styled "The World's Foremost Design Guru" in my publicity handouts. And that was how I was called by someone who asked me to be Artistic Director of the Millennium Dome. I accepted the challenge with alacrity: this was a project crying out for someone of my intellectual and aesthetic stature, and it would have been criminal to let it fall into the hands of a boring little bureaucrat or — heaven forfend! — a grubby little politico.

❖

All life, according to Nietzsche, is a question of taste. Schopenhauer, Wittgenstein, Plato, Popper: these, too, are philosophers who sit comfortably in one's prose. They have much of interest to say, in their own little ways, to the modern Design Guru. Sadly, though, as drivers they possess an all-revealing timidity. One may surely be forgiven for thinking that were Plato alive the poor little man would drive a Volvo S70 R with power steering, while it is inarguable that Schopenhauer would be stuck in a two-door Montego with a sun roof but without air conditioning.

Taste was what I wished to bring to the Dome. As I made clear to Peter Mandelson in my memo of acceptance, "Let me put your mind at rest. In appointing me Artistic Director, you have made an acute choice that does you great credit. Rest assured you have chosen a headstrong, brave, idealistic individual fired by intellectual and creative ideas, determined to banish any hint of 'populism', 'fun' and other vulgarities from the Dome, a true intellectual who is no slave to 'market-research' or — forgive me! — 'bums on seats'. Well done, Peter! I believe that, given time and a better dress-sense, you have the makings of a first-rate junior minister! Keep it up!"

❖

Our first meeting after my appointment was not a success. You may judge a man by his shoe-laces. I noticed as he walked in that Mandelson's were black, not dark grey. A ravine of displeasure opened in my head. Frankly, I shuddered. Mandelson's black shoe-laces immediately suggested that he had no interest in the visual, and that the Dome was doomed from the start. Did he not realise that black shoe-laces were last worn by the mercantile and clerical classes in the late 1960s, and have had no place on the shoes of the distinguished since late November 1962? The shoe-lace is a window into a man's soul. Anyone who fails to buy his shoe laces from Signor Maschetti's shop on the Via Garibaldi in Sienna is, frankly, not to be trusted with matters of importance.

To be helpful, I made this point crystal clear in the memo I sent him the next day. "I cannot continue to operate effectively in my new post" I began, "if I am to be forced to conduct business meetings with a man who insists upon continuing to wear black shoe-laces. I feel the whole purpose of the Dome project is jeopardised by this grotesque, lowering and unworthy decision. Reconsider the whole question of your intolerable personal presentation — or pray consider my resignation imminent."

❖

There are few shapes in this world closer to perfection than the oblong. I am generally credited with being the first person in this country — perhaps anywhere in the world — to have used the oblong to great effect. As long ago as June 1996 I was wearing oblong shoes and an oblong designer necktie, living in an architect-designed oblong house, using an oblong wok to stir-fry my oblong noodles.

I was determined from the outset that the oblong should form the basis of the Dome's interior. All other shapes were to be banned.

"I want nothing but oblongs!" I wrote in a major new memo to The Prime Minister shortly after accepting the post, "Big oblongs! Small oblongs! Medium-sized oblongs! Anything else would be philosophically incomprehensible, aesthetically compromised and morally untenable.

"I have therefore advised the on-site contractors to convert the at present hideously circular Dome into an Oblong, with eight different Zones, each celebrating the beauty of the oblong.

"Everything, even the food on offer to visitors, must be oblong. Pringles Potato Crisps must be awarded the catering franchise. This is a bold, brave and far-reaching initiative that is undoubtedly poised to attract the attention and admiration of the whole world. Finally, a word of design advice, Prime Minister, concerning your hair: an urgent appointment with Nicky Clarke is needed if you are to achieve anything worthwhile in your Premiership. If, for whatever reason, you choose to ignore this advice, I am afraid I shall have no option but to tender my resignation. Yours etc..."

❖

It was after I had threatened to leave if Philippe Starck was not brought in to design the lavatory-paper holders in the public conveniences of The Dome that the Government had the impertinence to accept my resignation. It then began to dawn on me that there is little to choose between New Labour and Hitler's Nazis.

• Both professed an interest in "The People".
• Both had only the most fleeting knowledge of Design.
• Both had leaders called "Tony".
• Both believed in world domination and set up death camps to do away with their political enemies. Chilling? Yes. Chilling like the rather splendid bottle of Chablis in the ice-bucket beside me. But then what would New Labour know about wine? Nothing at all! Touché!

RICHARD BRANSON

I was looking into a void. In all my life, I had never been so terrified. I knew at that moment that my future was in his hands. Would he make it? I watched his left hand stretch out. I held my breath.

No! He hadn't got there!

We didn't have long. Time was fast running out. I gasped inwardly as he changed hands and tried again. I knew then that this was our last chance. Slowly, slowly, his hand stretched towards its target. He faltered, and seemed about to collapse. Oh, my God! But then from somewhere he found one last burst of energy — and somehow he got there. Yes! He had made it! Keith Richards had managed to sign our multi-million pound 5-year contract!

Virgin was home and dry!

❖

Cool it, guys, just cool it! It's now over a year since her death. It's time we moved on. That's what she would have wanted. So let's just ease it a bit, right?

This was the message I delivered to the Queen and Prince Philip when I schlepped round to Buck P. for lunch two days ago. It was an informal lunch — thank God!! — so I didn't have to wear a tie or anything (yup, it's true, I really hate wearing ties — but that's just the kinda smart-casual guy I am! You won't catch me conforming — no way!). But I could tell just by the way they dressed and spoke that the Queen and Prince Philip were feeling a bit uptight. So I gave them a great big smile and some free advice.

I touched on many issues. Like how they should update the National Anthem. Did they know Phil Collins's great "Something in the Air Tonight"? Great song, great anthem — and sadly underused. And like how they should get a bit more contemporary in their dress-sense. "You'd look great in a pair of Virgin denims, ma'am," I said. "I'll get them sent round tomorrow, 40% discount." I then sat back and drew out a business plan for the Royals, peppered with the Virgin philosophy. Live for the present. Best foot forward. Swing low, sweet chariot. Buy low, sell high. You've gotta live life to the full. Every cloud has a silver lining. Pile 'em high, sell 'em cheap. A smile never hurt anyone. Every little helps. Tomorrow is the first day of the rest of your life. Love means never having to say you're sorry. Never mind the quality, feel the width...

When I'd finished, the head butler came over to my chair. He was wearing a tie. "Her Majesty and the Duke of Edinburgh send their apologies, sir, but they were called away twenty minutes ago. Did you bring a coat, sir?"

❖

Virgin Update... Virgin Update... Virgin Update...
Following hot on the heels of our highly successful Virgin
Rail division, next month sees the launch of our long-
awaited Virgin Nuclear Fuels. For too long, the whole
Nuclear Fuels thing in this country has been sadly lacking in
one essential ingredient — FUN. So, we've decided to take
our nuclear clients (yes, that's you, folks!) kicking and
screaming into the 21st century with a totally new, wicked
and updated service, including:

- Giant Smiley Faces on every Virgin Nuclear Reactor.
- Chris Evans lookalikes to supervise all onsite cooling
  processes.
- Two free tickets (back stalls and balcony only, all subject
  to availability) to The Rolling Stones World Tour 2002
  for every client contracting leukaemia or any related
  disease.
- Virgin Cola brewed under licence on premises for added
  fizz.

And, yes, to achieve some great publicity for what we
believe to be a world-class product, I myself will be
dropping the essential red-hot components of each Reactor
onto the Virgin Nuclear Sites from my world-famous Virgin
Challenger Hot Air Balloon. Yes, with your help, we at
Virgin fully intend to make it a boom time for the nuclear
industry! Great!

❖

I've always gone into business not to make money, but
because I think I can do things better than they've been
done before — and because I truly believe the public deserve
the very best, at the lowest price possible. Take Virgin Cola
— until I introduced it onto the market, the public had
never had the chance to buy fizzy black cola before. We had
a truly memorable launch. I wore nothing but a pair of

Y-fronts, then they painted me in the reds and blacks of the Virgin Cola label making me look just like an exact replica Virgin Cola bottle. At the appointed time, one of our splendid Virgin team put her hands on my beaming head, just like it was a bottle-top, and then proceeded to unscrew it. She then pulled my head right off and — whaddya know?! — out popped lots of bubbly sweet stuff! Another truly brilliant launch — and two per cent of the first day's take went to designated Virgin charities. Great!

❖

Virgin Update... Virgin Update... Virgin Update...
Next January sees the launch of Virgin Penitentiaries, our very own, cutting-edge contribution to Jack Straw's exciting new plans for taking the privatisation of the prison service into the 21st century. Every Virgin cell will be provided with its own special Virgin headset, with Mike Oldfield's classic Tubular Bells II playing 24 hours a day. And that's just the punishment block. Elsewhere, the VGLDs (that's Virgin Gold Lifetime Detainees to you!) will be able to while away their days with in-cell entertainment of an 18-hour loop-tape of classic Chris Evans banter, updated on an annual basis. Great for Virgin — and great for the country! Be there!

JULIE BURCHILL

It was the birth of the decade. Mine, I mean. I was born a brash beautiful babe, bawling and bouncy and bursting with bollocks in a big Bristol bospital. The angels sang their carols in their pukey middle-class choruses, there was a star overhead, and I was visited in my crib by poncey wise men bearing gifts. I took one look at them and thought, "Those toffee-nosed tossers make me want to throw up" and with one majestic flick of my forefinger I let them know what they could do with their wanky little gifts. Just one day old, and already I was slap bang at the dead-frigging-centre of the universe.

❖

Born a proud member of the working-class, I had no time for manky, moany, middle-class mores. School was pukesville. So I got a job on the New Musical Express. Talk about pukesville. So I married my first husband. What a tosser. So I became the highest-paid columnist in Fleet Street. Up your arse. So I married my second husband. Bor-*ring*. I hate all these wanky mediocre middle-class pursuits just like I hate the middle-classes. They're so bloody *fidgety* and full of *self-pity*.

❖

Within seconds, I was Queen of the Groucho Club. Every night, the rest of Soho would empty as I held court to my helpers and underlings.

"Tell us what you think of Mikhail Gorbachev, Julie!" one my little helpers would say.

"Oh yes, Julie, *please* tell us what you think of Mikhail Gorbachev, oh *pleeease*!"

"Fucking middle-class toss-pot," I would announce. "Bourgeois bloody baldy with a bog-standard birthmark on his bonce. Next!"

"We'd so love to hear your views on European Monetary Union, Julie!"

"Oh yes, *please* Julie, *pleeease* give us your theory on European Monetary Union!"

"European Moronery Union, more like," I would say, and my serfs would all gurgle with the pleasure of it all, filling their little notebooks with my sumptuous smorgasbord of startling sayings.

They would sit around me, my praetorian protectors, keeping me for themselves, cosseting me, guarding me because they didn't want anyone else to have me, Julie Burchill for I, I Julie Burchill, I myself was me and me alone, and what I knew was that I would always be me myself, whatever those up-their-own-arse self-obsessed solipsistic wankeramas sniffing their own armpits in the rest of the Groucho might mumble.

❖

One day, Alexander Solzenhitsyn walked into the Groucho. "It's that fucking beardie with the long face who slags off Stalin," I hissed to Toby Young.

"I'll bloody get 'im for yer, Julie!" said Will Self. "No one disses on your heroes and gets way wiv it. Lemme at 'im!"

"Biff him in the archipelagoolies, boys," I commanded them, "That'll bloody learn him to piss on Uncle Joe's hospitality."

But at that moment Charlotte R walked in. Suddenly, nothing else mattered. She plunged deep into the slipstream of my subconscious, and surfaced smiling, sleek with significance, supremely sauteed in a smorgasbord of sorcerous sensuality, shimmering with skintight savoir-faire, solemn as a scratchcard, spontaneous as soup, shadowy as the sun, saucy as semolina, scanty yet still sincerely and scandalously scintillating, with the shaming sense of sanctity of a shepherdess from Shropshire, or a saxophone — sexophone — played by Schopenhauer.

❖

Charlotte and I being mega-girls, and this being mega-love, we slammed the front door of our hutch and went at it like rabbits, thumping the ground, twitching our noses and gnawing on raw carrots. Not since Russia dropped the bomb on Hiroshima and Wham! broke up had the world seen anything like it. Suddenly, we were the most famous same-sex couple called Julie and Charlotte anywhere in the world. Regardless of our feelings, we would find ourselves ruthlessly splashed all over the bottom quarter of the middle-to-back pages in the early editions, providing we gave them reasonable notice and showed a bit of leg.

❖

My theory is that what the Seventies were to the Sixties, the Eighties were to the Nineties. Just as the Sixties were to the Nineties what the Seventies were to the Eighties. And from where I'm sitting in the Nineties, the Sixties was basically the Eighties, or an Eighties version of the Fifties, but with the Seventies coming in the middle. The Sixties was all bang-bang-Kennedy's-dead-boo-bloody-hoo-well-at-least-we-still-got-Keith-Richards and up until 1977 the Seventies was all Watergate-plus-Osmonds-and-Lava-Lamps-equals-Boresville, but then I came along waving my pen like Neptune's magic sceptre, and the rest of the Seventies was the Burchill Decade, just like the Eighties was the Burchill Decade with a bit of Madonna and Thatcher thrown in and the Nineties was the Burchill Decade, with my main rival Princess Di never managing to stick her foot through my door. But I'll tell you the worst thing about the Nineties. All those poxy little self-inflating columnists only ever writing about their own inky-stinky dinky little lives. Pu-*keeeey*.

BARBARA CARTLAND:
THE MEN IN MY LIFE

MAHATMA GANDHI.

I was introduced to Mr Gandhi at a party of Diana Cooper's.

I was perfectly frank. I informed him there was nothing very clever about parading around in a loin cloth drinking one's own urine and generally acting the giddy-goat.

As a result, he fell head over heels in love with me.

Men love to be told the truth, even when painful.

BENJAMIN DISRAELI.

I have never been attracted to men with facial hair. Which is not to say that they have not been attracted to me!

Quite the opposite! Before my marriage, I received proposals from over 29 men with moustaches, 17 of them sporting beards as well.

The gifted novelist Anthony Trollope once asked me to marry him, and so too did the famous Benjamin Disraeli, just one of 8 Prime Ministers who have fallen head-over-heels in love with me.

The famous scientist Charles Darwin, the highly respected composer Johannes Brahms and the tireless philanthropist Father Christmas all begged me to accept their hands in marriage.

But I thought they could all do with a jolly good shave.

So under a star-filled sky, with the moon as bright as can be, I waved them goodbye to the distant music of Cole Porter.

KARL MARX.

But Karl struck me as different. We met in the Embassy Club.

Everyone else was dancing the cha-cha, but Karl was buried in a book.

Like many Germans, he was a bookworm, and awkward with women.

"Don't tell me!" I said, interrupting his reading, "You're going to ask me to marry you!"

He looked up and introduced himself. I could tell — don't ask me how, but we women can — that with just one glance he was already head-over-heels in love with me.

He told me he was working on a book called Das Kapital. I was perfectly frank. "No one will want to read a book with a dreary title like that," I said. "And tell me, Karl, how does it finish?"

He told me it finished with the workers owning the means of production. I knew then that he was making a most ghastly mistake.

"It must have a happy ending, Karl. The man in uniform must kiss the gorgeous young beauty, and ask for her hand in marriage. I will write it for you!"

Call it instinct if you will but I knew Karl thought it a brilliant idea. But when the book came out, I found to my horror that the publishers had omitted that final chapter of mine.

The book consequently enjoyed only limited sales.

I was dreadfully disappointed for Karl. I am told that he is very out of fashion these days.

Whereas my own books are still read by thousands of millions of people the world over.

CAPTAIN HOOK.

Others may have found him tiresome, but Captain Hook was always frightfully sweet to me.

It was a moonlit night. A piano was gently tinkling somewhere far away.

"You are so very lovely, my dear," he said, "And I do so want to place my arm around you."

With that, he placed his right arm around my shoulder. Alas, his prominent hook, never his strong point, caught the strap of my brassiere and then with a resounding snap unloosed my ballgown.

I stood naked on the dancefloor.

Among the assembled onlookers were the Governor of the Bank of England, Lord Beaverbrook, the Duke of Devonshire and the Admiral of the Fleet, all of them interesting people.

Before the tune had drawn to an end, all four of them had requested my hand in marriage.

I never saw Hook again, but I will always remember him as someone rather special.

SIR WINSTON CHURCHILL.

The 2nd World War was a beastly business. I am often credited by my many admirers with having won it single-handedly.

Certainly, my natural beauty, my charitable works and my gift with a pen did much to pull this country through.

But credit should also go to Sir Winston Churchill, the Prime Minister at the time.

Winston was one of the most interesting men who ever met me. When he talked, I simply had to listen. Unless I had something more interesting to say.

He said many memorable things I now forget. But among his words of wisdom were these.

"Barbara," he said, "If it weren't for your matchless beauty and your brilliance with words, your insights, your charity work and your abundance of goodness, the ordinary men and women of Great Britain would not have had the stomach for the fight."

It was a charming thing to say. I might have married him, but he was married already. Divorces can be awfully messy.

EARL MOUNTBATTEN.

Most people know that Earl Dickie Mountbatten was head-over-heels in love with me, that he was one of my dearest, oldest friends, and that we were planning to write a book together.

But few now remember that he was also the Supreme Allied Commander of the South East Asia Command and the last Viceroy of India.

He was a brilliant inventor. He invented the bow-tie, the motor-car, the Catherine Wheel, the jet-engine, the escalator, the telephone and the soda-siphon.

Always dashing, Dickie once took me for a ride in a motor-car he had just invented. Whereas other motor-cars sped along dangerously, Dickie's remained in one place for hours on end. Brilliant Dickie!

Dickie would often drop by to try on some of my gorgeous dresses and fabulous ballgowns. But he gave me a few jealous looks when I appeared in the marvellous pink outfit with satin bows he had earmarked for himself.

Needless to say, I stole the show.

JEREMY CLARKSON

Talking of ugly places, I think most reasonable blokes would agree that Venice *just about takes the biscuit*!! Talk about revolting! I've seen prettier things crawling out from under a stone in an Essex sewer!

All that water, for instance! What's up with the Venetians, then?! Don't they know the first thing about road drainage?!!!!!

And I've never seen so many truly *dreadful old* buildings! Haven't those Italians ever heard of a nice lick of Dulux Emulsion Gloss?! And have you ever tried riding in a gondola?! A new-range SAAB XPG convertible it is not!

But what really bugs me about Venice is the total lack of cars! So you want to drive your brand new Jag SR6X with super-roll suspension and tail-lights to get any bird horny enough to give you five blow jobs in under the minute around the streets of Venice? Sorry, pardner, *no can do* — or as the spaghetti-guzzlers would no doubt put it — *"nonny! nonny! nonny!"* Yes — Venice is just about as ugly as my old gran's hairy armpit!!! City of Beauty? More like City of My Bloody Arse!

❖

Okay, so let's talk about Oranges. Yup, that's right — the so-called fruit. I've gotta come clean. I Don't Like Oranges. There — I've said it! To me, the orange is just about as disgusting to eat as a dog's turd — and believe me that's *really saying something*!

For one thing, oranges are *so bloody ORANGE*! And they're so bloody *ROUND*!! Honestly, you'd think by now they'd've hired themselves a decent designer to make them square or *RECTANGULAR*!

And what about all that juice! Come on, girls — admit it! It reminds you of a bloke having a truly great time!! Yeah — that really puts the ORRR! into ORRRANGE! Let's talk to the head of The Orange Marketing Board!

Clarkson: So what do you think of my views about oranges, then!!! Pretty bloody *controversial*, eh?
Head of the Orange Marketing Board: Ha! Ha! Ha!
Clarkson: Are you honestly telling me that some people actually *LIKE* oranges??!! If an orange was an animal, it would be a *SLUG*!! And if an orange was a breakfast cereal, it would be one of those ones that *sticks to the bottom of the plate even after it's been washed up*!!! And if an orange was a fruit, — it would be an *ORANGE*!
Head of the Orange Marketing Board: Ha! Ha! Ha!
Clarkson: Thanks for letting us hear your worthless opinions! Great! You've been a good sport! Great!! Now go away!! Great!!!

❖

So finally I get to do a bit of your actual straight-up-and-down honest-to-goodness steady-as-she-goes your-place-or-mine motoring. It's the new Bluebeard HRT that's waiting for Clarkson today, and from the look of her she's positively raring to go, like a Dutch airhostess, brunette, hair done up in plaits, full lips, pert as hell, who's been stuck on trolley duty since Bangkok.

You ain't seen nothin' yet. Oh boy. You can say that again, mate. In my twenty-year career in motoring, I've never seen nothin' like this babe. Let me tell you this, if this car was a woman, she'd be on her back and gagging for it before you could say Peugeot CDM.

I lollop hard down on the shaft-neck, strike the fuschia into suction, drag on the marrowbone and before I know it I am clocking up fifty aspidistras on the zimmer. Slam on the footstool, into third and then it's easy on the old scrofula. The underwench is looking good, the V-neck is great, and one glance at the thrombosis tells me the entire Preston Candover is pure state-of-the-art.

Into fourth, and it's basting the turkey all the way. The grasshopper's pulling on my left leg, the scavenger is coming along nicely, and all that's between me and the road is the well-cooked sprout. Boy, is this one hell of a sexy hedgehog!

I'm up into fifth now, giving it the full aspirin, and the baby's mewling like a woodlouse. Heavy on the camiknicker, and she's taking the corner like a bantam. You can forget all that stuff about the antelopes, because this lemon-squeezer could shuffle a six-pack and still have change for a scarecrow. Phew — and to think I might have left my duck-warbler in the snuffle-shank.

❖

Why does cricket go on so long?
Why are mobile phones so irritating?!

How come when you drop a piece of toast it always lands on the buttered side?!

Have you ever noticed that the Italians take one helluva lot of care over their appearance — are they all gay, or what?!

Say what you like about the Queen, but I wouldn't do her job for all the proverbial tea in China!!

Has Geri Halliwell got big boobs — or what??!!

It never rains but it pours!

And believe me, too many cooks really do spoil that broth!

But my main controversial opinion this week concerns Shoes. Yup — *shoes*! Those horrible little things you wear on your feet! Some have laces — and a fat lot of good they are! And others are called "slip ons" — for the simple reason that if you leave them lying around you are bound to "SLIP ON" them!!! And they're no good for anything other than putting on your bloody feet! Have you ever tried wearing one on your head? You haven't? Well — don't try it, mate! Big mistake!! It quite simply *won't stay on*!!! Awkward little buggers, shoes. Have you ever noticed how dirty they get if you step in mud? Well, have you? Yet we're always being told how clean they are! Fat chance!! If a shoe was a world dictator, you can bet your bottom dollar it would be *Saddam Hussein*!

This week, I got my own back on Shitty Shoes by buying a whole load of them and then throwing them one by one into the wood-fired ovens at my local Pizza joint. Blimey, mate — you shoulda seen that *blaze*! And what about them French then — all garlic and onions. *And they don't even speak English*!!!!! And Shakespeare! What a load of old rubbish, eh? And Mozart! Urgh! Give me Dire Straits any day!

Great! Lovely! Smashing! How did I do?

MATTHEW COLLINGS

Not such a bad place to start really

You've got to start somewhere. So it might as well be here. But is here better than there? There might be just as good. OK, let's start there. It's probably just the same. Only different.

What's it all about then?

Hi! Me again! I've just written my first paragraph. The one beginning "Not such a bad place to start really". So that's one less to write. And to read. But we're still a long way from the end. Of course, you could skip. But that would be breaking the rules. Or is breaking the rules what it's all about, nowadays, in the modern world, now? Hey!

This is Modern Art

Whoops! Forgot to tell you. I'm wearing my art critic hat now. This is me. This is my take on the world. This is my journey into nothingness and back again via something. Or other.

Yup.

I'm a pretty crazy kinda guy.

So let's talk about art. Three letters. A. R. and T. It's not tar. It's not rat. It's not tra or atr or rta. It's art. So what's it all about then?

Look at this:

.

Now look harder. You're probably saying, "Hey! That's just a full-stop. I've seen one of those before!"

But that just goes to show how stupid you are. This particular full stop is a scale copy of an original created by the major conceptual technominimalist Hans Orff in his warehouse in Detroit. Orff has been creating full stops, some of them over twenty yards in diameter, for the past twenty-five years.

Orff's full stops are black. Very black. As black as the blackest bit of black, or even blacker.

And they are circular, like the world.

And that black, black circle says a lot about death, it says a lot about modern anxiety, it says a lot about our whole concept of what kind of concept a concept really is, it says a lot about everything and a lot about nothing. And it says a helluva lot about the here and now.

Hey! Let's take another look at it:

.

It could be an eye. It could be an arsehole. It could be the void. And it could be a crazy modern world spinning out of control. Either way, it's shattering. Or something.

In fact, it reminds me of a full stop created by Samuel Beckett in Krapp's Last Tape. And another one created by Alain Robbe-Grillet in Look Up Name Of Difficult French Novel And Put It In Later.

It says a lot about the impossibility of saying a lot. And it says a lot about the impossibility of saying a lot. Whoops. I just said that.

Or did I?

Just about halfway now

I went to the opening of the new installation by Gary Bowgus. The room had six cars in it, all shiny new and pointing outwards, as if somehow desperate to get into the fresh air, to escape into — what? — the big outside. But they were prevented from escaping by a huge sheet of glass, stretching from the floor to the ceiling, right along the front of the room.

The cars were empty. But they all had steering wheels. It seemed to me to be a very, very powerful statement about our modern world, its surfaces, its feel, the sheer look of it, about the thinginess of things and the carness of cars, about the way we are all steering towards something yet at the same time we're not even behind the wheel, a very good, very nice, very good, whoops said that, very real comment about the singularity of single things, almost playful in its intensity yet at the same time childlike in its conceptualisation of post-ironic distance.

"Excuse me, sir."

It was the Commissionaire, interrupting me as I was taking my notes.

"If you want the art gallery it's next door. This is the car showroom."

Wow!

What Is Gillian Wearing?

It's shocking because it's real. And reality is what we're avoiding. Where's that thought leading me now? It's leading me to Tracey Emin, the undisputed leader of radical radicalism in the second half of 1999.

Matthew: Tracey, this looks really interesting. I like its texture, its colour, the way it catches the light. It's telling me a lot about the aboutness of about. But what exactly is it, would you say, how would you put it into words?

Tracey: It's, like, dental-floss. And it's used. Basically, Matthew, it's a piece of, like, used dental-floss. Burp.

Matthew: To me it has an incredible, almost dental sort of flossiness to it. What's it saying, then? Well, to me, it says a lot about floss and a lot about dentals. It reminds me of early Velazquez, who also dealt in teeth, yet it's still very much in tune with nowadays. It asks questions about the past like, "When did I last floss my teeth?" and questions about the future, too, like, "When will I next floss my teeth?" Blimey! I'm trying to get my head around all these questions about time. Tell me, Tracy, this whole question of time, what's the next big question you're going to ask about time?

Tracey: Intit about time you pissed off? Burp.

Almost finished

The year: 1999. The time: now. The place: here. The mood: up-to-the-minute. You're thinking, "Has he run out of things to say?" And I'm thinking, "Yeah, right, I have." And that's a perfectly good question and a perfectly valid response.

Sit back. Enjoy yourself. Play an old Velvet Underground record. Chill out. Be cool. Grab yourself a glass of Tequila. Hang loose. No worries. Ask the big questions.

Yeah, baby: This is Modern Art.

JOAN COLLINS & FRIENDS

"How on earth do you keep your skin so fabulous? Do tell!" I was chatting to one of my very dearest friends, the infinitely glamorous Ivana Trump.

"You know, Joan," she replied, pouring me another cup of Mascara Herbal Tea, which darkens your lashes as you drink it, "I think the greatest beauty secret of all is love. But you have to love yourself first, because unless you love yourself you can't expect to be loved in return."

"That's so true, Ivana!" I said. I learnt to love myself thirty years ago and I've never looked back. My husbands have been the beneficiaries — all four of them, five including the next one, six if you count the one after. "But tell me, Ivana," I continued, lovingly, "how on earth do you manage to hide all those broken veins, darling? You are brilliant!

From this distance, one can hardly see them at all! And, believe me, you have the most fabulously toned *derrière* I've ever seen on a woman over sixty."

"I'm thirty-nine, darling. Have a top-up!" replied Ivana, pouring another cup of herbal tea over my lap.

• *JOAN'S TOP TIP: The Hunza Tribe from the Himalayas are known for their longevity. Their secret? Clarins Cocoa Butter Skin Firming Gel with a Dior Foundation.*

Angie Dickinson, a fellow Gemini, has achieved incredible harmony in her life. Two personal trainers, three children, four husbands, five houses, six face lifts. "You still look gorgeous, Angie, even though you've put on a bit of weight since I last saw you! Just how do you *do* it, Angie?" I asked her, casting an admiring eye over her chins, both absolutely perfect. "Let us into the secret of your beauty routine! It must be pretty extensive!"

"My skin is quite dry, Joan," she replies candidly. "So, my health consultant has concocted a special recipe. Beat two eggs thoroughly and apply the mixture to your face and neck. Add a rasher of bacon and a grilled tomato. Rest for twenty minutes while they harden, then pour on a cup of lukewarm milky coffee, Costa Rican for preference. Now add a mug of cold porridge and keep it there for five hours. Then, if you are attending a top Los Angeles brunch party for glamorous high-fliers, you can simply lie down on the trestle table and let guests serve themselves."

"That makes so much sense, Angie! Now tell me your basic philosophy of life. Is it, by any chance, 'My body is my temple. Come all ye hither, and worship'?"

"But first, Joanie," says Angie, "Please, please, *please* tell me how you get that fabulous bloodshot effect in your eyes — or are they naturally that red?"

• *JOAN'S TOP TIP: Even if you are poor, fat and ugly you can still have a great time. Below-stairs jobs can be marvellously rewarding — and you might just get to meet a fabulous superstar from one of TV's leading mini-series!*

For over four decades now, Shirley Bassey has been one of Britain's most enduring stars. At well over sixty years old, she is still able to almost fill the smaller auditorium of the Empire Ballroom, Swansea. Her diehard fans, many of them now in their late seventies and early eighties, hang on to her every word as she yells her way through a shattering medley of her three hit singles, a stunning reminder of the Sixties, the decade in which she first became a grandmother. From a distance and in the right light, she really doesn't look a day over sixty-seven.

"Why is it, Shirley," I asked, "that so many young people today go out without make-up? Whatever happened to family values, Shirley?"

Shirley adjusted her eyelashes meditatively. At just five foot three inches, her 170 pounds are exceedingly well distributed, particularly in the area of the upper arms. "They simply don't know the meaning of the world glamour," she agreed, taking out her hand-mirror and discreetly wiping her lipstick off her front teeth.

"What I think is desperately sad is the end of glamour on TV," I continued, while Shirley readjusted her gorgeous wig so that it made room for her expensive nose. "Shows these days leave nothing to the imagination. Tastelessness, vulgarity and coarseness are the order of the day. Where's the mystery, where's the magic, Shirley? One longs for the golden days of real entertainment — shows like 'Dynasty', 'The Bitch' and 'The Stud'."

"You know what my motto is, Joan?" replied Shirley, helping herself to another serving of ice-cream with added sun-block. "My motto is 'Never forget to dental floss'." And with that, this gorgous, vibrant lady takes out her teeth and gives them a jolly good going-over.

• *JOAN'S TOP TIP: Remember to look after yourself after death. To look really polished, your skeleton will benefit from a bi-monthly application of deep-cleansing moisturising cream from Laboratoire Garnier. And the great thing about being dead is that it lets you cut down on fatty foods and maintain a gorgeously trim figure!*

Shirley Maclaine and I go back a long way. The first time we met, I was married to Anthony Newley, and she was going out with my second husband. The next time, she was going out with Anthony Newley, and I was going out with her brother. The next time, her third husband was going out with my second husband, her brother was going out with my first husband's wife, Shirley was now married to my fourth husband, and I was in the process of divorcing her fiancé. Through it all, neither of us abandoned our hard-won belief in old-fashioned family values.

Shirley is an intensely spiritual person. For her, inner peace is not just a matter of the right lip-gloss. It requires repeated applications of Fabiella eye cream. "I've been a mystic since I was very small," Shirley told me. "I believe we are all on a journey into our own search. The search for inner peace, Joanie, is all about life energy and centring yourself, so that you come to realise we have been here many times before, and your mother was once your own daughter and..."

But by this time I was late for my appointment with the gorgeously-preserved Betty Bloomingdale, so I crept out and left her to it — an amazing, life-enhancing woman never more interesting than when talking to herself.

SIR TERENCE CONRAN

You know, I find the whole processing of food —
slicing, grating, cutting, stirring, nibbling,
masticating, imbibing, savouring, swallowing,
digesting, expelling, wiping, flushing and then slicing again
— enormously satisfying. I take enormous pride from the
fact that in the 1950s, I became the first Briton to visit
France. In those days, the avocado, the tomato and the
potato were quite unheard of in Britain. I take enormous
pleasure in having introduced them to this country, where
they now form part of our everyday lives.

I crave simplicity. Good restaurants are all about
simplicity: simple food, simply served with simply
enormous bills.

For instance, what could be more satisfying than a simple
boiled egg? Ever since, as a young man, I became the first

Englishman to visit Europe, I have pursued a love affair with the boiled egg. A boiled egg is a feast for all the senses: the eyes amazed by the deep rich yellow contrasted with the stark, translucent, almost virginal white; the ears alive to the gentle knock-knock-knock on the warmly curvaceous and softly yielding shell; the mouth teased by expectations of the flowing yolk softly easing its way along the salivating contours of the tongue, and down, down, down into the throat; the penis quivering in readiness to be used as a spoon, diving deep, deep, deep into the very nub and hollow of the ovoid, then rising up once more, now drenched in brightest yellow. And it's also quite nice with toast.

❖

I think I am right in saying that I was the first person in Britain to develop a passion for good design. But what enormous opportunities were missed by the generations who preceded me! The River Thames, for instance, has many major design faults, and is long overdue for a corporate makeover in order to radically alter public perception of it as something "outdated" and "worn out". We have accordingly developed a three-point Thames Re-Imaging Plan:

DESIGN PROBLEM: The Thames curves randomly, without due regard for the sadly outdated buildings alongside it. This is bad design: fussy, obtrusive, and lacking the "human dimension".

DESIGN SOLUTION: Radically re-design the Thames, banishing all fussy curves to form a marvellous bold and simple straight line, in a stroke making it user-friendly, democratic, gutsy, passionate and ready for the new demands of the 21st century.

DESIGN PROBLEM: The Thames is far too moist and splashy. It is made up almost entirely of water, creating an almost insuperable access barrier between the North and South of London, making it wholly unfit for pedestrians.

DESIGN SOLUTION: Tile the Thames in richly checkered Italian tiling, terracotta and a marvellous deep lush green, blocking out the water and allowing full pedestrian access, affording it a marvellously "continental" street-market feel, full of marvellously evocative bustle and hub-bub.

DESIGN PROBLEM: "The River Thames" is a tired, yesterdayish log, too strongly associated in the public perception with a lack of vibrancy and drive. It is crying out for a radical re-think in its corporate identity to reflect its new, all-dry, user-friendly, updated competitive edge.

DESIGN SOLUTION: A new corporate identity for an old River, radically altering perceptions with a dramatic new logo, incorporating a go-ahead new one-million-pound designer typeface that is impacting for change:

*tha**M**es: t*he *ri**V**er*

❖

I am an enormous supporter of the new Prime Minister, Mr Tony Blair and New Labour. And I always have been, ever since the 80s and 90s when I used to have to really clench my teeth whilst heaping wholly undeserved praise on Mrs Thatcher and Mr Major. But I trust this new Government will give long overdue public recognition to the importance of British Design — for example the Butler's Wharf Development, the Bluebird Emporium, the new Conran Group market repositioning of Hadrian's Wall with a tremendously exciting Mediterranean-style bistrodome every 750 metres. New Labour (and I do enormously urge them to go one step further and become neW labouR) has a better understanding of the importance of design to the economy and quality of life. I trust they will soon take this initiative one stage further by appointing a major Design presence to the Upper House. The whole design community would benefit enormously from, say, a Lord Conrad of Bibendum to lend real buzz to their cause.

❖

As I've said before in many major newspaper profiles and countless exclusive forums for leading politicians and businessmen, I am not a remotely ambitious man, not a bit of it. I'm easy come, easy go. I hate that ghastly expression "control freak". I have consequently banned it in all my offices, shops and restaurants.

Frankly, I prefer the simple pleasures of life: eating, drinking, the company of friends. But of course one does have to get them *just right*, there's no point having any-old-friends, a terrible mish-mash of different sorts of people saying different sorts of things in different sorts of ways. With friends to dinner, one desires above all else perfect simplicity. My perfect dinner party would consist of five close friends, three women, two men, the women between 5ft 4ins and 5ft 6ins, the men rather taller, between 5ft 10ins and 6ft 1ins, the women in black and white classic Chanel, the men in pale green hand-stitched linen suits with bold red ties, the table matt-black and chrome with petrol blue banquettes, the lighting controlled electronically from three lines of continuous rooflamps, the highly-polished stainless steel ashtrays repeating a central motif of the overall design echoed also in the door-handles, the conversation a closely-monitored balance of long, short and medium-sized words. Ever since, in the early 1950s, I became the first Englishman ever to travel abroad, I have made it my business to extract the most enormous pleasure out of life. I'll be designing tomorrow's plans for pleasure extraction today — copies of instructions, layout and group targets to all relevant employees, two copies to senior executives and accountants.

MARGARET COOK

Actually, I feel very, very sorry for him. He's looking so old and wrinkled and unhappy these days! Urgh! For his sake, I only wish it hadn't turned out like this!! I only wish I hadn't had to inform the world that he's a self-serving, cheese-paring, paranoid little toad who's so randy he'd leap on his own granny in her grave if he could only get his hands on a shovel. It's a desperately miserable situation for him!! And with so much at stake!!

But it's Gaynor I feel really sorry for!!! It really doesn't seem fair on her, poor love!!! Just when she's settled so nicely into Chevening, with all her lovely new dresses and everyone on the verge of forgetting she's just another jumped-up little secretary who got her claws into her boss, poor Gaynor's had to discover through reading the Sunday newspapers that she's actually shacked up with an alcoholic weasel who spent most of their courtship plotting to leave her. I'll never forgive myself if she leaves him!!!!

❖

It was 12.26 on June 9th 1992. The day before, Robin had confessed to me he was having an affair with my new horse, Randy. But after drinking two bottles of Remy Martin, he had vowed never to see Randy again, other than at essential gymkhanas.

As I understood it, we were both keen that our marriage should surmount these obstacles, but over breakfast the next day Robin had involuntarily let out a whinny before cantering around the kitchen in search of coco-pops. He had temporarily forgotten he was no longer in the stables. It was a grossly insensitive act, but for the sake of our marriage I chose to ignore it.

It was sunny, so we decided to go for a picnic to patch things up. But as I was packing the sandwiches, Robin suddenly snapped. "That hamper! Look what colour it is!"

"It's... brown," I said.

"Brown! Brown!" he yelled. "Yet you know how Brown is trying to frustrate my career at every turn! And he's a complete nobody! Future Chancellor, my foot! I know more sums than him! He can't even do six threes!... And he's not even Scottish — he just puts on that accent. Everyone knows he's really a Pakistani! Oh, Margaret, Margaret — how could you torment me so!"

At this point, the phone rang. "Oh Tony, how super to hear your voice!" said Robin. "Margaret and I were just going out for a modest picnic in your honour! And how's the lovely Cherie? Super! What's that you say — a fairer tax system, taking more money from the poor to give to the better off? Sounds great to me, Tony! Cheery-bye! Big kiss!"

After he had put down the phone, Robin looked as

pleased as punch. I suggested to him that in order to get on, he had sold his soul to the devil. "But he gave me an excellent price for it," he replied, triumphantly. I could tell he was buoyed up by the way he was unzipping his trousers. "Tony said I was doing an *excellent* job," he commented. He then leered in my direction. "Any chance of a shag?"

❖

Robin could be desperately insensitive, without a thought for the feelings of others. So I was determined that the rest of the world — not forgetting our young lads — should know all about it. After all, it's not every young man who has a drunken lecherous has-been for a father and a devoted and discreet public servant for a mother!

Throughout our married life, I struggled to keep it all secret. These are just one or two of the things I tried desperately to keep my sons from finding out. I'm thinking of the day Robin rushed into the house, sat down on the cat, swigged from a bottle of cooking sherry, broke wind and started singing bawdy songs about Peter Mandelson. I'm thinking of the way he would behave like an ostrich, racing around the room on two legs wearing nothing but a feather boa, his neck outstretched, desperately trying to fly. And I'm thinking of how his memory began to have gaping hiatuses induced by drink and sleeping pills. Out of the goodness of my heart I once told him he'd been Prime Minister for the past six months following the death of Tony Blair. The look of joy on his face was a thing to behold!

❖

On May 19th 1997, Robin came into the room wearing a school cap and shorts and sucking his thumb. I could tell at a glance he was putting on his little-boy act. In this mood, he was prone to boasting. "Actually, I'm not having an affair with Pamela Anderson," he said, out of the blue, "But I could if I wanted to. *So there*!"

By this, I judged that he wanted me to think he *was* having an affair with Pamela Anderson, perhaps so that in this way he could make me feel guilty that I did not have a starring role in TV's "Baywatch". But I rose above it. "That's nice for you," I said.

"*And* I could be Foreign Secretary one day if I wanted to," he continued, "'cos Tony said so."

I said nothing. I just continued to peel the sprouts.

"And Pamela Anderson says she would love to welcome foreign dignitaries with me. And at the same time she thinks she could get me a part as a lifeguard on Baywatch, which Tony agrees would greatly enhance Britain's reputation at home and abroad, and..."

I let him go on. Two hours later, I found him flat on his back in the toilet with his trousers round his ankles and a brandy bottle at his side, his right hand still twitching a little as it attempted to draft an opposition amendment to the Tory Government's latest white paper.

In describing this scene, I have been as gentle as possible. One doesn't want to hurt his feelings — after all, there's no telling how touchy he gets! I haven't mentioned, for instance, how The Rt Hon Little Robin Diddums once confessed to having had a brief fling with our pet hamster, Totty, or how he secretly placed a "Kick Me" sign on Gordon Brown's back as they emerged from a Shadow Cabinet meeting or how he always keeps a six-pack of Special Brew in his... You see, that might endanger his future career as a senior backbencher. And that's the last thing I'd wish to do.

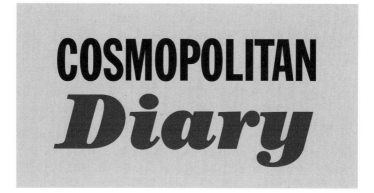

COSMOPOLITAN
Diary

I t's a well-known fact that we women positively *hated* sex until *Cosmo* came along and taught us all how to get the most out of it. Now, thanks to *Cosmo*, statistics show we're enjoying MORE and BETTER orgasms than ever before. 'Scuse me for a sec. Oooooyeeehaaah! Whoopsy, there goes another! And I didn't even move from my desk! FAB! Here on *Cosmo* we have them *all the time*!

With your orgasms in mind, we're delighted to bring you, free with this issue, *The Cosmopolitan Book of 253 Sensational Positions Around the Home*. For instance, have you ever tried having sex with your guy in a tumble-drier? Or in a chest of drawers? Or on the glass shelf in the bathroom where you put your toothpaste? You haven't?!! No wonder you're so fat and you've got spots and nobody wants to do it with you!

Cosmo Arts: Zero orgasms in Ian McEwan's HOT NEW Booker contender — but it's still a tender and titillating MUST READ. Huggy Bear MARTIN AMIS has a new book of SHORT STORIES out — and you know what they say about men with SHORT STORIES! Finally, the new JOHN MORTIMER is a cool, very papery 325 pages long — talk about COMING out in HARD back!!

Find your V-spot. Here on COSMO we're all having orgasms all the time from our G-spots, our A-zones, our C-zones and our T-spots. Been there, done that — bor-ing!

But have you found your V-spot yet? We all have!! How to find it: go right inside, first right, second left, round the corner and straight on, you can't miss it. But don't worry if you can't find it: you're probably one of the 2.01% of sad women who just don't know how to have fun.

Cosmo's 6 Ways to Become Really Rich and Famous:
1) Change your hairstyle and lose weight so you look just like Nicole Kidman. Then wait until she is in her dressing room at the Donmar Warehouse, lock the door — and take her place on stage! The critics will go wild — and you'll get to go home with hunky Tom Cruise!
2) Become a White House intern by filling in the FREE form in next month's Cosmo — then give a sensational blow-job to the Vice-President of the United States! But first lose weight!
3) Find out which glamorous five-star hotel Hollywood heart-throb George Clooney will be checking into on his next visit to Britain. Lose weight, do something about those flabby buttocks, cut down on fatty solids, and apply for a job as a chamber-maid. Then when you know George is soaking his HUNKY body in the bath use your skeleton key to burst into the room! Taking care to first

remove your clothes, leap into George's bath with him —
and exit as the soon-to-be 4th Mrs George Clooney! But
remember — the Hollywood paparazzi can be intrusive:
avoid all hassle by keeping the exact location of your star-
studded wedding a closely-guarded secret known only to
you, George and your new best friend, the fabulous
Roseanne Arnold!

Diet News... Diet News... Diet News... Experts at a
Colorado-based institute have discovered that 100% Full Fat
Ice-Cream eaten in HUGE quantities can make you PUT
ON THOSE INCHES. So if you want a body like Naomi
Campbell, cut back on that extra Cadbury's Flake and
remember to go for THE ONE-SCOOP OPTION.

Food News... Food News... Food News... Sexiest food on
the market? You guessed it! Mmmmmm! It's the LATEST
100% Full-Fat Vanilla and Strawberry Ice Cream with
EXTRA chocolate chip cookies! Apparently, top model
KATE MOSS is totally HOOKED ON IT and she and top-
shag boyfriend heart-throb superstar JOHNNY DEPP eat it
ALL DAY EVERY DAY. Kate reveals that slurping it
down gives her a guaranteed extra 101 orgasms a day — and
it's also a great way to lose weight!

Serious COSMO Issue of the Month: Proportional
Representation. A commission on electoral reform under
Lord Jenkins of Hillhead reports next month. This is a
serious issue, which could effect the future of our
parliamentary democracy. But is changing the voting system
a good idea? In a word, do we really want a first-past-the-post
system? Or would we prefer to lose a bit of weight, gorge
ourselves silly on a super-sexy tub of vanilla ice-cream and
have 62 orgasms a night with the fabulous Ewan McGregor?

3 Ways to Boost Your Lifestyle if You're Stuck in a Dead End Job Reading Self-Help Lists:

1) Save those boiled sweet-wrappers! Sellotaped together, they could make a FABULOUSLY REVEALING baby-doll negligee similar to the type worn by Bubbly TV Personality Anthea Turner before her bust-up with BOYFRIEND GRANT.

2) Impress your friends! Fill your fridge with magnum bottles of WHITE'S LEMONADE and saucers groaning with HEINZ BAKED BEANS! With one glance, friends will IMAGINE you are enjoying a CHAMPAGNE AND CAVIARE LIFESTYLE!

3) Gripfix a lifesize pin-up of sexy Robert Carlyle to your boyfriend's head, make him escort you to a top celebrity party at the HOTEL SAVOY — and see heads turn!

HEY YOU! STOP WORRYING! If you're falling short of the national average of six (6) orgasms per sex-session and nineteen (19) sex-sessions per week — don't worry! It probably means that your boyfriend doesn't fancy you very much after all — so perhaps you should think about losing a bit of weight and getting a new boyfriend. Or are you a closet lesbian? It doesn't matter if you are, really it doesn't, not these days! But DO remember to RELAX and STOP WORRYING — particularly if you haven't REDECORATED YOUR SITTING-ROOM for six whole months (and you REALLY wonder why you don't have as many friends as you used to?!!). And what's that ODD SMELL in your bathroom? Hey, STOP WORRYING! Just lose weight, change jobs, get a new man, have yourself a makeover, get a new wardrobe — and BE YOURSELF!

CHRIS EVANS

Chris: I tell you wot. Phew-WEEE! Okay, right! Yup! Let's get this sorted — sorted let's get this, okay! This is the world's most intelligent-io breakfast show, presented by *moi*, Mr Christopher Evans, coming to you LIVE through your tranny and all that stuff — woooh! But that's enough talk from me, let's see what the team have to say, okay team? I said, okay, team?

Little Man Helper: Hahahahaha! Great, Chris!

Little Woman Helper: Hahahahahaha! Reeely great!

Chris: That's more like it, ha ha! So let's talk about what we all got up to last night. What about you, little woman helper?

Little Woman Helper: Hahahahahaha! Reeely great!

Chris: How's your bazookas today, love? Bit sore after a mucho heavy bitty-bit of bouncy-bouncy last night, ha ha?!

Little Woman Helper: Hahahahahaha! Great Chris!

Chris: Not half as heavy as I got up to with an unnamed MEGASTAR whose name I am not prepared to divulge! By the way, did I ever tell you I once went out — and I'm talking DOING IT — with the famous Kim Wilde! Did it with her ooodles and nooodles of times! Blimey! I tell you wot, she didn't half turn it on, did our Kim! Should've seen her in the nuderisimmo! Talk about bazooming bazookas! Should've seen 'em, really should! But that's strictly private, strictly, strictly private, it was just something very private and personal and beautiful between me and the lovely Kim, and I think it would be quite wrong to reveal on air exactly where the lovely lady in question let me put my twelve-incher — wayhayhay, what about that, team!

Team: Hahahahahaha! Great, Chris! Hahahahaha! Reeely great!

Chris: Blimey, I tell you wot, the amount of beer I had last night down the pub with some good mates, and I didn't throw up once, not once, but then if I had I'd've just got someone to clear it up for me, cos I'm that rich, I really am, I could even pay someone to clear it up with their TONGUE!

Team: Hahahahaha!

Chris: And get it off tax! No, but I could, honest; honest, I could. I tell you wot, my contract with Branson, right, it's like worth millions and millions. Mega-millions, right? Anyway, the phones've been going wild ever since we bin on from listeners saying I'm worth every friggin' penny of my millions and millions 'cos there's no one like me, Chris Evans, no one at all, and Branson should give me

more if he wants to keep me, and there's a fax from
Jeannie in Derbyshire offering to pay me five grand just
to suck my —

Team: Hahahahahahaha!

Chris: Put it this way, this lady wants her tongue to go
where Kim Wilde's and hundreds of others have gone
before. Now's the time to unzip my bank balance and
waggle it in the air, darling — it's the biggest you've ever
seen! Hahahaha!

Team: Hahahahaha! Great Chris!

Chris: Coming up, in forty-five minutes we got a pop song
for you, so you can nip out for your wee-wees then —

Team: Hahahahaha!

Chris: — but before that I tell you wot we got some fan-
mega-tastic talk from me coming up, with amazing totally
new things and stuff to learn about my own good self,
Mister Christopherrrrr Evans, like what brand of lager I
was supping with me good mates down the boozer last
night, and what I think the Chancellor of the
Exchequeroomi, thingy, you know, come on, come on,
like, yup, wosisname, then? —

Little Man Helper: Brown.

Chris: Tha's the one, Graham Brown, what I think the
Chancellor should do about the Monetary Union, but
first I wanna — Break That Wind!

Team: BREAK THAT WIND! Hahahaha!

Chris: Yes indeedy, it's that time of the morning —
WooooHoooo! — when I personally "Break That Wind"
out of my own B-T-M — that's short for arse! — down
through the airwaves and out through the radios of all the
ordinary little people like your own good selves at home
or driving to work! That way, every single person in the
whole world can boast to each other they've personally

heard Chris Evans break wind LIVE on British radio that very morning! Yeserooni! So let's hear the chant, team!

Team: Break that Wind! Break that Wind! Break that Wind!

Chris: So heere goes. Stand back, everyone:
PHWRWRWRWRWWRWPFLPFLPFLPFLP!

Team: Hurray! Great, Chris! Hahahahahaha!

Chris: Woooh! Tha's better! Like, I should be paid an extra two and a half grand, maybe three, for that! Not as easy as it looks to let rip live on air, y'know! Yup! Yeeh-hah! Okay, right! You know wot. So where were we? Thassit. Yup. Major question. Chancellor Graham Brown and what he should do about the European Monterararararary Union. Chuck it, Graham! Tha's my advice! Who wants bloody ECUs anyway? Not me, and tha's for sure! I got millions and millions of pounds anyway, all written into my contract! So stuff it! Tha's wot we say, innit, team?

Team: Yeah! Hurray! Great, Chris!

Little Woman Helper: You're so great with your opinions, Chris. You should be a world leader, right?

Chris: Did I ask you to speak? Did I? Well don't bloody speak 'less you're asked or you're out. Hahaha! Cheers! That's that sorted then. All right then. Yup. Like. Woooh! Love the stuff! Tell you wot, where were we, right, yeah, here's a question for everyone out there: If you had to have sex with a rodent, which rodent would it be? Mouse? Rat? Hamster? Budgie?

Little Man Helper: Er, Chris, a budgie's not a rodent, ha ha!

Chris: I don't need that from you. Out. Now. Piss off. Look, like I'm the star of this show, I'm the one with the contract, and if I say a budgie's a rodent then a budgie's a rodent, right? Let that be a lesson. Hahahaha! Great!

Team: Hahahahaha! Great, Chris! Great! Great! Great!

MOHAMED AL FAYED
WITH HIS TRUSTY PR
MICHAEL COLE

Mohamed Al Fayed: Before we fakhin start, let me say I thin man, okay, very, very thin man. They say I fat, my enemies they say Al Fayed fat, I not fat, my enemies fat, they all fakhin fat, I tell you why they fat, they fat because they eat my Harrods food hall fakhin goodies I give them free, that's why they so fakhin fat. But Al Fayed is thin, you tell them he thin, Michael, you tell it like it is, you straight the fakhin record set, fakh them pigshits.

Michael Cole: Through the good aegis of your columns, may I point out that Mr Mohamed Al Fayed, whom I have known and admired for many years, cuts an exceptionally svelte figure as he glides on tip-toe through the many luxurious Harrods departments distributing gifts to the poor and needy. Far from his being on the "plump" side — a malicious and potentially libellous rumour put about by his enemies, many of them now languishing in gutters, Mr Al Fayed is admired throughout the world for his remarkably lean quality. A couple of historical facts — attested on record by four prosperous witnesses, including a distinguished nightclub bouncer, a leading figure in the world of debt enforcement and the owner of a chain of highly-regarded casinos in Swindon and surrounding areas — must serve to get the record straight.

Now aged 47, Mr Al Fayed can look back on a career which saw him capture the title of Most Beautiful Male Body in the World sometime in the early 1970s, somewhere out East. His waist — measured regularly by leading statisticians — now comes in at a sprightly 28in — remarkably thin for a man of his age (45). Only last month, at a reception for Harrods' new gold-embossed Vertical Take-Off Jump-Jets at Kensington Palace hosted by the Princess of Wales, paid for by Mr Al Fayed, catering by Harrods, the Princess — looking never lovelier in an off-white ballgown with satin fringe — swept up to Mr Al Fayed and gasped, "Mohamed, poppet — you must be the thinnest person here! How do you do it?"

Mr Al Fayed's enemies deep in the heart of this corrupt Government may have suggested that recent photographs show a significant bulge at waist level beneath his exquisitely-tailored Harrods own-brand suits. I am told these photographs may have been doctored at senior level by MI5. I do not know. But what I do know is that Mr Al Fayed often wears clothes for the fuller figure so that he may hide Harrods gifts there, for later distribution to crippled children, his photographic schedule permitting.

Mohamed Al Fayed: Yeah, you tell em fakh off, fakhin pigshits, bad people, terrible crooks, show them Al Fayed is sophisticated man, he know how to write swanky, real swanky, commas, stop-fulls, the lot, and you sign that letter "Yours fakhoffly Mohamed Al Fayed". I say fakh them all, that's what I say.

I like the Queen, nice woman, very nice woman, very good friend, for me is diamond you know, is jewel, she no bullshit, if she hear word against Al Fayed she say, "You can fakh off you fakhin shit, Mohamed good man, Mohamed my friend."

God Save the Queen, and He will, Al Fayed tell Him to, He take many gifts off Al Fayed, God owe Al Fayed favour. Queen very nice lady. So how much she cost, Michael? We talking day-rate here. I want Queen at Harrods sharp for 9.30 opening, I want her on perfume counter, I want her modelling latest fashions, I want her in soft furnishings, I want her on fakhin sausage counter in food halls, all time with Mohamed beaming at her side. What she ask for that? Help her image, too. People no more say, "She lazy fat bitch that Queen, she no do nothing just take bribes", no, people say, "She work with her hands, she common touch, Majesty friend Mohamed, is good." You write fancy fakhkin letter to Majesty, Michael, tell her get round here snappish or it's finito for the Palace, okay?

Michael Cole: *"Your Majesty, It is my most heartfelt hope and wish that you should honour my humble Harrods Department Store of Knightsbridge with your gracious presence at your earliest convenience, theretofore extolling the delights of the very best of British commerce to the world at large, all proceeds to charity. I remain, Ma'am, ever your most humble and obedient servant, The Hon. Mohamed Al Fayed, OBE.*

"P.S. I enclose a Gold Voucher, redeemable for a three-night

midweek stay for two, at the Le Ritz Hotel, Paris, meals included, no questions asked, Range Rover to follow."

Mohamed Al Fayed: Shit-hot letter, my man. Everybody want take Harrods from me, fakh them, but not with Queen as hostage, no way, Queen nice lady, Queen my sister. Fakhin Establishment — pwah! — they crook, they bad person, I spit on the graves of their mother, they think Al Fayed not posh, that what they think, I tell them what I think, I think Al Fayed he posher than lot of them, he know how to talk proper, he know manners, he fancy dresser, no need buy their fakhin shit. You tell them that, Michael, you write letter from Mohamed to top people's paper, you tell them, Al Fayed no need your Establishment crap, he better born than lot of you, fakh it.

Michael Cole: *"Sir, Many harsh things have been said about me, but it is cruel beyond measure to imply that I am in any way seeking acceptance by 'the British Establishment'.*

"Why should I have need of such blandishments? I am first and foremost a family man, and a Royal family man at that, being first cousin of her Majesty the Queen, and a blood relative of over six hundred different Dukes and two thousand English Earls. Following extensive blood-tests by accredited physicians, my wife has established beyond question that she is a half-sister of HRH Princess Anne, as well as first cousin of the Princess of Wales. Furthermore, my solicitors possess signed statements from reliable witnesses to the effect that I am not only Honorary Chairman of the Garrick Club and Master of Trinity College Cambridge, but also, without wishing to boast, Her Majesty's Lord Lieutenant of Scotland. With all this, who could want more?

"Yours faithfully, Lord M. Al Ponsonby-Fayed (39), Harrods, Knightsbridge."

RICHARD E. GRANT

JABBERJABBERJABBERJABBER. When actors get together, we YAK. WOOOOO-FUCKING-WHEEEEE, don't we yak! I guess it has something to do with the strain and TENSION of being someone other all the time. So we talk ourselves back into real life, comparing combat notes like 1st World War soldiers coming back from the trenches, tough and urgent.

"Loved your Withnail," says John Malkovich.

"Thanx," I say. "Loved your Liaisons."

"Thanx," he says. "Loved your Withnail."

"Thanx," I say. "Loved your Liaisons."

"Withnail," he says, changing the subject. "I just loved you in that."

We jabber on like this for hours, getting to KNOW one another, blood-brothers in fantasy.

❖

Message in my hotel pigeon hole from Martin Scorsese.

Martin SCORSESE!

MARTIN Scorsese!

MARTIN SCORSESE!
MARTIN SCOR-FUCKING-SESE!

I feel betwixt myself with joy. He tells me he loved me in Withnail. Me?! He loved ME! I stutter something about loving everything he's ever done. "I just wanna say I thought you were GRRREATTT!" he says. In a mad moment, I think to myself that it's time I showed I don't just KOW-TOW to everything he says, to show that I'm a bit of a fucking REBEL, so I take the plunge. My stomach wrenched with fear and courage I seek to contradict him. "NOTHING like as GREAT as the way you directed TAXI-DRIVER!" I say. "You're a FUCKING GENIUS!"

At this point, we establish eye contact. His eyes sear into mine like heat-seeking missiles. Uh-oh. Have I gone TOO FAR? Have I thrown away my BIG BREAK by being TOO HONEST? Scorsese pauses, pulls on his beard. Then he says: "And you were great in 'The Age of Innocence', too."

MARTIN Scorsese!
Martin SCORSESE!!
MARTIN SCORSESE!!!
Marty.

❖

Acting's a dreamerooni, so I always try to get my feet back on the ground after a hard day's sweat on set. I meet close friends for a drink and talk about ordinary down-to-earth things like acting and films and future roles and so on. Tonight, I relax over a drinky-fucking-poos with Uma Thurman and Gary Oldman. We exchange views on Sean Connery and Julia Roberts with Tim Robbins and Val Kilmer, who are staying with Lauren Bacall, who told them she just loved Withnail — very humbling. Later, I need a bit of exercise and meditation, so I walk down Sunset Boulevard with Steve Martin, and we quietly share our euphoria about, among other things, Marty S. and Dan Day-Lewis and John Malkovich. Just then, a young boy comes up, looks at Steve and says, "JEEEEZ! You're STEVE MARTIN!" and asks for his autograph. It hits me with a jolt that these people — ordinary guys, personal friends of mine — are seen as so SPECIAL STARS by members of the public, who love to DROP their NAMES! How odd people are, and what a bizarre, upside down, crazy, wobble-inducing world this Hollywood stuff really is. I determine to tell this to Barbra Streisand if ever the day comes — JUST THINKING ABOUT IT MAKES ME GASP FOR BREATH — when I am privileged to meet that SCREEN-BLOODY-GODDESS.

Woozy-on-down the street — STRIDESTRIDESTRIDE — just walking along, like an everyday person in this city of drea-fucking-ms, yakyakyaking with Steve about the other, that and this. It's one of those magical, hope-filled, fine and gorgeous, yet not really so fine and gorgeous, with an undertow of banality and pessimism, LA-ish sort of LA days, very LA yet with its own kind of particular feel to it that's not really LA at all but yet which also is LA: there's an indefinable SOMETHING to it that's definitely not LA, but not LA in a very LA-ish sort of way. In many ways, it's one of those EASYPEASYLEMONSQUEEZY kind of days when you want to drag someone into your heart and tell them what's REALLY ON YOUR MIND.

"Did I tell you I just loved 'The Man with Two Brains'? We've got it on video," I say to Steve.

"Did I tell you Victoria and I saw Withnail twice, no, nearly three times?" says Steve.

We walk on in silence, the raw emotions of two human being reverberating into the winds like leaves on quite a windy day.

❖

Sit down on my ARSE with a new script. The part was originally scheduled as a tough-guy role in the Scottish highlands for Sean Connery but then he sprained his wrist while waving at someone with his hankie and it was rewritten as a vehicle for Bette Midler as an over-the-top dancer in LA but then Bette — who's reportedly seen me in The Player *three times* and loved my performance — had to pull out so the role was re-jigged for Gene Hackman as the commander of a U-Boat in the 2nd World War, with Bruce Willis as the torpedo. But Gene and Bruce were busy working on a new vehicle for Sean Connery, "The Invalid", so the role was totally re-thought with John Malkovich in mind, playing a tormented artist with a frown — perhaps Tchaikovsky or Van Gogh, depending on soundtrack availability — but John finally couldn't do it because he'd had an accident with his frown, so the script — now about a comical overweight Victorian housemaid, lands on my desk. "I WANT THIS BRILLIANT LITTLE FUCKER!" I think as I finish the script, "IT'S AS IF THIS PART HAD BEEN WRITTEN JUST FOR ME — I'VE GOTTA HAVE IT!".

❖

Another day in the studios, another walk on the tight-rope between hope and despair. I sit around like Hamlet in the play of the same name, not knowing quite what to do, or how to do it. I am playing a tall, thin man with wild blue eyes. How the fuck am I going to play him? I WRESTLE with the problem for two — three — four minutes. Then I decide to play him TALL and THIN with eyes that have a kind of BLUEY WILDNESS about them. I take my idea for the role to the director, Bob Altman (BOB ALTMANNN!!!!), who saw Withnail twice and loved it both times. He looks at me with both eyes, as only a world-class director can. His eyes are like blackcurrant milkshakes or billiard balls or more accurately two eye-like orbs on either side of his face, bold yet liquid, fearsome yet sympathetic, and in the final analysis very, very *eye-ish*. "I like it," he says.

HE — LIKES — IT! I'VE CRACKED IT!
EU-PHUCKING-PHORIA!

GERMAINE GREER

For Chrissake, the hypocrisy out there is so gross that sometimes I can't BREATHE. As one of the only women in this godforsaken country permitted to nurture her own land, I know this only too bloody well. 58% of men disapprove of women who garden, and another 49% positively hate them. Only the other day, I was in the vegetable patch, placing condoms on the aubergines for greater protection from the devastating east wind, when to my horror I heard a buzzing noise coming from my hat. I then discovered that I had a bee in my bonnet, for God's sake, and I couldn't get rid of it. To my amazement, the manufacturers had failed to place any hole in the bonnet for the bee to exit through. This is because manufacturers of women's headwear rejoice in women being stung, so that they can then hand them over to doctors, who can in turn torture them for no better purpose than the enactment of control.

❖

And another thing — the stone in my shoe. It's been there for six months, for Chrissake, and no one's done a bloody thing about it. Every time I put my shoe on, there it is again. In our "enlightened" society, women are indoctrinated not to complain when there's a stone in their shoe. Instead, they're forced to choose between a stone in their shoe — or a stone in their shoe. What kind of choice is that? At the end of the Millennium, there's simply no choice, stonewise. It makes me very angry — and I'm darned if I'm going to take it any more.

❖

It doesn't take a genius to guess that the electric toaster was designed by a man. Why? Because it's lousy for putting in the dishwasher. Every time I put my electric toaster in the dishwasher, it fucks up, and I have to go out and buy another one for Chrissake. For 92% of men, the dishwasher is merely a means of irreparably damaging toasters, leaving their wives to toast bread by hand, leading to 33% body burns, and bogus research suggests that a further 17% have attempted at some point in their married lives to stack their wives in a dishwasher before turning the knob to Rinse. It's even been said that women are sexually turned on by the dishwashing cycle. Oh yeah? This kind of made-up statement makes me hopping mad. How DARE anyone give it the time of day — let alone repeat it in print? How DARE they? And any woman who has tried boiling fresh organic vegetables in a household toaster by pouring in the water, throwing in the veg and pressing down the button will have been brought face-to-face with a world eco-system primed to destroy their self-confidence. Even in 1999, 98% of those who still wear dresses are female. Just think about it — and SEETHE.

❖

How many more times do I have to say it, for Chrissake? Women of a certain age are totally ignored by the British media. We are forced to endure endless hardship, grief and pain, our mouths ruthlessly gagged by a world system balanced against us. I've said it over and over again — on Question Time, The Late Show, an Omnibus Special, on Radios 1, 2, 3 and 4, Newsnight, in every newspaper from the Mirror to the Telegraph and on a 6 part series for Channel 4 — but do they listen? Do they heck.

❖

Close study of my farmyard geese has taught me an awful lot about men. Before I studied geese, I had no idea that men were so totally obsessed with waddling about, moving their necks to and fro and quacking all the time. This is real and pervasive and obvious. Not until we have stopped men behaving like geese will we able to call ourselves fully human.

❖

At the end of the Millennium, contempt for the mother has assumed a new dimension. In Hitchcock's movie "Psycho" the hero dresses up as his mother before performing his/her murders. In the Tintin books the mother of the eponymous hero is totally and damningly ignored — in over 17,500 pictures, spanning 23 books, she never once appears. On Brookside, the mothers tend to be older than their daughters, and in the recent movie of The Titanic, we are repeatedly reminded that the heroine is not a mother, and thus — it is cruelly implied — all the more worthy of our admiration. Meanwhile, scores of mothers are thrown overboard and drowned. Male psychologists from the University of Makeupname tell us that men would make much better mothers — but then they would, wouldn't they? For Chrissake, I've spent a lifetime travelling this vast universe of ours, my feet clad in nothing but shoes, in search of a mother who is accorded her proper respect. I say a lifetime, and it would have been a lifetime but for the repeated and WHOLLY UNNECESSARY, DAMMIT interruptions from my selfish, useless, carping old ma in Sydney. SHUT YOUR EFFING GOB, MUM! Doesn't she have any thought for others? Doesn't she realise I've got important work to do? Who the hell does she think she is? Frankly, I've got nothing but contempt for her type. It's time to get angry, very angry.

❖

The penis is suffering from a severe personality disorder. Once it was admired, even coveted, by women, but now it's an object of pity and contempt. What's it FOR, for Chrissake? It's no good as a tent-peg, and useless as a hoe. Those who have tried using it as a chimney-brush have been bitterly disappointed, and it is quite simple unable to withstand the heat for stirring soups and casseroles. Like 79% women, I can no longer be bothered to find house-room for the penis. Women of the Ohokeykokeykoki and Tararabumdeeyay tribes of Central Africa have taught me that it can make an effective table decoration on those long winter evenings. I might try it next year. Through their peasant wisdom, we arrive at contentment.

❖

Together, we feminists can change the world. Our values are sanity, calm and a profound connection with the earth. Together, we can make this world a better place, a world of unity and companionship. But I'm not talking about you, Fay Weldon. Or you, Natasha Walters. And certainly not you, Suzanne effing Moore. And you can piss off too, Ros Coward. And you. And you. And you. Thanks for bloody nothing. Is there no one other than me who's prepared to do as I say? I guess I'll have to promote unity all by myself, then. God, it makes me ANGRY. Men!!!

AN AUDIENCE WITH
ELTON JOHN

(Applause. More Applause)

Elton John: Whoo! Yey! Thank you mother! Hey! Great! Great! Thanks guys! Thanks for giving me the clap — whoops! Ha ha!

(Audience laughter. Applause. More applause)

Elton John: Any quest-ee-o-nez? Anyone want to *draw me out*? Whoops! Put it back in, man! Oi! Oi! Ha! Ha!

(Laughter. Standing ovation)

Elton John: Do we have the Spice Girls here tonight? We do! Yey! Lovely surprise! Ginger Spice — Do you want to come down on me with a question — whoops!!? Ha! ha!

Ginger Spice: Elton, we all love your classic rock songs and we think you're a true Spice Boy, but —

(Cheers and applause)

Ginger Spice: — but what we'd like to know is, what was the most memla, the most, er, membub — er, what was it?

Posh Spice: Memrurboow.

Ginger Spice: That's the one. The most memrurboow night of your life, Elton?

Elton John: OOh-er! Pass the vaseline, mother!

(Laughter and applause)

Elton John: Seriously though, it was probably that time when John Lennon —

(Applause. Tears. Lights lowered. Standing ovation)

Elton John: Thanks. Great. That time when John Lennon came onstage with me and it just really was one of those truly great evenings and together we sang the song I'm gonna sing for your now, with great lyrics by Bernie, and like you say it was a truly memorable evening.

(Applause)

Elton John *(sings)*: Ah kint explain, woh noh, There's somethung abaaht the weeay Yoow luk tonaaaaght!

(Applause. More applause)

Elton John: Woooh! Yey! Great! Thank YOU! Do we have Chris Evans in the audience? We do! Yey! Chrissie baby! Ladies and gentlemen, the great Chris Evans! Woooh!

(Applause. Laughter. More applause)

Chris Evans: Yes, Elt! Well, Elty baby!

(Laughter. Applause)

Elton John: How you doin, Chris? You can spin my CD any day — it's a whopper! Ha ha!

(More laughter. Applause)

Chris Evans: Elton, you've been a major star in this great industry on both sides of the Atlantic for twenty-five years now. Looking back, I think what we'd all like to know is who is your totally fave current breakfast dee-jay?

Elton John: Chris — no one comes near you. Truly! And you've got a lovely arse, mate!

(Laughter. Applause)

Elton John: Seriously, I'd like to sing for you now a truly memorable song, which I remember truly from the days when I had true memories of myself as a lad, and, like everyone, singing along with it — and let me tell you, it was truly memorable. Abide With Me.

(Applause)

Elton John *(sings)*: Abard wiv meey.

Yaba-ard wiv meeeeey

Yabaaard wiv meyeyeyeah

Ya-ba-AAAAARd weeEEev meeeeeyah.

(Tears. Applause. More applause)

Elton John: Do we have a question from Janet Street-Porter? Where are you? Ullo, luv!

(Applause. Laughter)

Janet Street-Porter: My oi ars yow summing personaw? Air big's yaw cock, ven? Ar Ar Ar!

(Laughter. Huge applause)

Elton John: Ha ha ha! Great! Ha ha ha! Twice as big as your boobs, dear! Ha! ha! ha!

(Audience cries with laughter. Applause)

Elton John: Touche! Ha! ha! ha! Bollocks! Ha! Ha! Ha!

(More laughter, cheers)

Elton John: Seriously, though. Mister Graham Taylor! Graham?

Graham Taylor: Chiz, Elton. Elton, how come you such a great all-round bloke plus triffic sensafuma?

(Applause)

Elton John: Thanks, mate. Seriously though, I love everything about Watford, and all those great guys there cos they all so grounded, they just treat me as a todally ordinary bloke, which is what I am, they just treat me todally normal, like one of the family, like they say, hey, Elton, loved your last single, or hey, Elton, mate, your TV special was todally outasight, mate. No fawning, nothing, just straight up, one bloke to another. And I todally appreciate that, I really do.

(Applause)

Elton John: And this is a song from my new album, Normal Bloke. *(sings)*:

Ler-er-erv is all we gard
I say, ler-er-erve is all we've gar-ar-ard
An if we gut ler-er-er-er-erve
Then ler-er-erv is all we gar-ar-ar
Ar-ar-ar-ar-ar-ar-ar-ar-ar-arrddd.

(The audience stands. Applause. Cheers. Catcalls. More applause. More cheers. More catcalls. Tears. Kisses. Waves. Hugs)

ERICA JONG

Yes, I've always loved words. Long words. Short words. Middle-sized words. Words not exactly short, but still not quite long enough to be called middle-sized. In-betweeny kind of words. No matter. I love them all. As a child, making words slant across the page was like making rain. Hey! I could make rain! The revelation impacted on me like a triple orgasm on a deck-chair. See the flowers bloom under my golden rays! And isn't that a rainbow athwart the pastures? Beneath the arbour of the corn-bush, a young rabbit pleasures an older one with his twirling, tinkling, rabbity tongue. The older rabbit has taught him all she knows of love, and now he is repaying her in full. Fill me! Fill me! Yes, I was the God of all I wrote, and, like God, I was going to change the world.

And so I did. Just two years after I wrote "Fear of Flying," Richard Milhous Nixon resigned from office. 12 years later, with the publication of "Horny as Hell: The Feminist Diary of an 18th Century Lady", Nelson Mandela was released from prison. And almost exactly eight and a half years after I wrote "How To Save Your Own Life", the Berlin Wall came tumbling down. This week, I have a new book out, and, whaddya know, a new Millennium is soon to be announced.

❖

"To be or not to be," wrote the acclaimed playwright William Shakespeare, "That is the question." My thoughts entirely.

❖

A book is a kind of hand-grenade, throwing water into the air like a dove nibbling at seed. My novels set up chain reactions all over the world which, believe me, I can't control. An image comes into your head. You set it down on paper. And the world is never quite the same again. Though I am world renowned for my powerful and influential brave and sexually-explicit novels, I see myself primarily as a poet, like W.B. Yeats or William Wordsworth, but much more in tune with the needs of the modern woman. Like them, I am obsessed with death, but I also enjoy my purchasing power, brought about through a hugely successful career as a thinker, poet and novelist, translated into over thirty-two languages worldwide and favourably reviewed in many of our leading journals. This poem came to me while shopping. It's called "At Macy's".

Death
Profound. Eternal. Unknown. Arriving at
The end of life like an
Unhurrying penis saying hello
To nipples that will do anything

For his autograph. Is that a settee in
Velveteen-lycra mix over
There? Like death, that I
<u>*Must have.*</u>

❖

I did not know Diana, Princess of Wales, very intimately.
I never met her more than a dozen times. In fact, I met her
less than a dozen times. A whole lot less. To be frank, I
never met her at all. But fate was to fix the Princess and the
Poetess together for all time. My life and hers ran parallel.

The coincidences were uncanny. We were both women,
and English was for both of us our first language. We both
had christian names that ended in "a", and though her
surname wasn't Jong, it was something close, and, like mine,
had an "n" near its center. We both had blonde hair, and
were adored by many millions of people. Diana had two
sons, and I had a daughter. I had written over a dozen
highly acclaimed best-sellers that had changed the lives of a
generation, and Diana had written nothing. Diana was still a
virgin, and I was basically still a virgin, maybe not quite,
but hey, who's counting? The same day Diana walked down
the aisle in St Paul's, I was sitting in my apartment in
Manhattan, watching her on NBC, woman to woman. Our
lives were already inextricably intertwined: we were like
two sides of the same coin.

The more I learnt about Diana, the more I felt I knew
her. Like me, she was a Jewish girl from Brooklyn. Like me,
she was crazy about Emily Dickinson and Pablo Neruda,
hot for sex in the sun-soaked morning of a Venetian
afternoon, three times divorced, a sucker for fellatio with
gondoliers and the victim-to-be of a world still suspicious of
the woman as artist.

And now Diana is gone and I alone remain, an icon for us
both, a woman the media wish to burn as a witch at the

stake of their forsaken dreams. I am Oscar Wilde, Dante, Emily Bronte, Sylvia Plath. I am the Delphic Oracle, the paradox eternal. You can't see it? Then maybe — just maybe — you haven't yet confronted the reality of being a woman.

❖

Ah, *Venezia!* (the Italian for Venice). It is like no other place on earth, a city blessed with having been the lustrous, historic setting for one of my most memorable novels. *Venice*! Though it rhymes with tennis, there are few tennis courts there. But it also rhymes with Penice or Penis. Ah, *Penezia!* To me Venice has always been a young man, his chest rippling with muscles, dragging me to his bedchamber, nimbly unbuttoning my *Versace* top, pulling out his manhood and slowly yet urgently entering me again and again and again, like the little man in a Swiss weather predictor on a changeable day, full of bright spells and blustery showers.

Let me paint a picture of Venice in words. Plash, plash. Laughter wafts across the canal. Fragments of conversation float under my open window. Plash, plash, plash. Beneath my silk *blouson*, my nipples sway to the gentle hum and thrust of the *canale*. Only the occasional plash-plash-plash of an oar interrupts the silence. Plash. There it goes again! Plash-plash! And again! The air is aromatic with the scent of coffee. Soon you are transported to a world in which the gentle lapping of your lover's tongue against your breast takes you to a — plash! plash! plash! plash! plash! — hey, is there no end to this infernal plashing?! Quit this plashing NOW! Room SERVICE! Oh, someone shut the fucking window, can't you, this fucking plashing's driving me *maaad*!!

JAMES LEES-MILNE'S
HEAVENLY DIARY

P ass away and go to heaven, much over-rated but not without its modicum of somewhat fanciful charm. The golden gates, written up in such hushed tones by the guide-books, prove a tremendous disappointment: garish, garish, *garish*. How one longs for a little English *restraint*. Instead, one must suffer the iniquities of the worst excesses of Italian bravado. Alas, they are largely Romans up here; homos, too, I shouldn't wonder.

❖

Am met at the gates by St Peter. Like many a bearded man, he is rather too full of himself, with an excessively *beery* air about him. One would have thought that by now the greeter at any halfway-decent club would have been persuaded by the powers-that-be to take a razor to his chin.

St Peter welcomes me warmly, but there is far too much touching and — *one shudders to think of it!* — Christian names all round. He is scruffiness personified — not only the hairs sprouting out from every orifice but the lack of any collar or tie. It all reminds me of a cocktail party given by Mrs Foley in Eaton Square in early 1947 to see the Stoke Edith needlework hangings in her drawing-room: quite well done and perfectly civilised, but unkempt, disordered and somehow *louche*.

❖

After the formalities — name, profession, date of death, and so on — one is introduced to this angel and that, none of them particularly forthcoming. They speak in hushed tones of Satan. I seize my cue. "Not one of the *Yorkshire* Satans?" I say, but I draw a blank. It is only too obvious that they have no idea. I remind them that, in the chilly autumn of 1933, I spent a delightfully wicked weekend with Sir Cecil and Lady Cynthia Satan at Damnation Hall, just outside Scarborough. Once again, they contrive to look nonplussed. I suspect them of stuffiness, though I have sufficient manners to refrain from mentioning the feathery protuberances that spring so unashamedly from their backs: *wings indeed!* The sure sign of a homo; quite possibly a wop homo at that.

The Angel Gabriel makes an entrance. He smiles in the sweetest, kindliest way, so that I immediately fall head over heels in love with him. He positively *sparkles*.

❖

To a harp concert, quite well done and some pretty passages, but the audience ugly and unwashed. "Who let *them* in?" I ask the Angel Gabriel. It emerges that they are all *bona fide* inhabitants of Paradise. "Come one, come all," explains Gabriel, all goatish and playful. Hardly a suitable policy for admission, I remark. Some sort of means by which one could separate the educated from the smelly would surely be preferable. Paradise is no place for savages, I add, casting a lizard-eye in the direction of an unshod fellow got up in a dirty brown cape, covered in creepy-crawlies and fluttery things. "But that's St Francis of Assisi" interjects Gabriel. I stand corrected.

❖

Off to the clouds, to an intimate *soiree* to meet my fellow new boys. The very sight of them fills me with gloom. Left-wingers abound, ghastly people voicing noisy, modish opinions — all faith this, hope that and charity the other. To my horror, I am introduced to a squat little woman, no taller than an umbrella, her skin coarsely lined and burnt to a crisp, all in all a slightly *chinky look*, her unimpressive and ill-laundered robes dishevelled and riddled with dust. "And who let *you* in?" I felt like hissing, just as Gabriel informed me that she was known as Mother Teresa (of *Calcutta*, of all places!). If this is democracy, God help us. "Do you happen to know Debo?" I ask, in a vain attempt to break the ice, "Oh, but you should! She's an absolute *treasure*! Chatsworth is very heaven. Or heaven sans *riff-raff*, if you follow me." M. Teresa looks back at me with a look of gormless incomprehension. Oh why on earth does one *bother*?

❖

At last, I find myself with an *entree* to God the Father. His house may indeed have many mansions, but to my eye every one of them is fearfully *declasse*. I fear it would have been rather more accurate for the scribe in question to have declared that His villa had many chalets. The furniture, too, is not up to much. Nevertheless, I take pains to persevere through the ghastly piped music of the assembled harpists, and attempt to set God at his ease. After much struggle, I make a little headway. "It's awfully noble of you to allow so many of what one might call the Great Unwashed into your

Kingdom," I venture, "But have you ever considered the benefits of the long red rope? We found them a tremendous boon at the National Trust for cordoning off the more, shall we say, *private* areas of a Home from those who would have little or no idea of how to behave within their confines. Needless to say, I would be only too pleased to oversee any cordoning-off programme you may care to initiate."

Just as I am getting into my stride, an archangel bangs a gong and announces that dinner is served. At last, I arrive at the front. "Big Mac, Filet-o-Fish or Chicken McNuggets?" asks the presiding Angel. I fear there may have been some awful mistake, and I have been sent to the wrong place.

MEG MATHEWS &
NOEL GALLAGHER

MEG: A lot of my time is spent organising and stuff. Like, Noel and me really like watching the soaps and stuff, but we haven't got time to watch them all, so like most people we employ a personal soap-watcher to take notes and someone else to type the notes up, and like a personal videoist to video the best bits, a personal editor to edit them down, igsecra, igsecra, personal projectionist, igsecra, igsecra, then this week to top it all I've had to conduct a range of interviews with applicants for the post of coming round with the ice-cream tray in the middle — and then you need the personal cleaners to pick up the cartons and spatulas you've left round on the floor and stuff. And someone's gotta scrape the pizza off the seats and — you got it — it's me who's gotta find that someone. And still the tabloids claim I just lie around doing nothing and looking really great! Durrh!

NOEL: Our kid Liam won the Patsy this year, not bad goin', our kid. Liam put on his outdoor gear and went up to collect his Patsy in a televised fookin ceremony in front of all these stook-up tossers, like he was really wound up by them. But there was all these other rock stars queuing up for their Patsy, and that really wound him fookin up, so he starts swearin' and smashin' the place up an' that. Now he's returned his Patsy in disgust, as a gesture against all those other fookin blokes who've had one. So I gets my genius to thinkin about this and I've come up with this fookin great song, best fookin song in the whole history of the world ever. It's called "Patsy" and it goes like this:

Yeeaaah, Patsy
Don't be nasty
You're bein' hasty
Treatin' me like a rat — see?
That would be ghastly
Yeaaaah, Patsy
You're lookin' pasty
Have some more pastry
Don't go astray
On me, Pat-seeeeee!

Fookin genius, and all to a tune just like Lady Madonna, but with fewer chords. And you can tell it's a great fookin song because like if you look at the last words in every line they fookin *rhyme*, see? And next year I'm gonna be up for a Patsy myself, 'cos unlike our kid Liam I'm fookin *sophistercated*.

MEG: Oasis are recording a really great new song, "Hey June". It's not just a totally searing howl of pain, it's also a terrible indictment of everything we think we know and don't and quite a lot we think we don't and do and a fair bit we think we don't know and in fact really don't know in the capitalist world of Thatcher's Britain. Noel's lyrics are truly superb:

"Hey June, don't make it bad
Take a sad song and make it better
Remember to let her into your heart
Then you can start to make things better
Na na na na na na na, na na na na na"

I leave the studio utterly numbed at this painful cry of anguish at the lives of young homeless people on the street in our inner cities. There must be something we can do for them, right. I vow to ask Noel tonight to like sign five hundred autographs, cos that way we can get them to my special events secretary for distribution among the needy in time for Christmas. And then another idea comes — we'll hand-pick some really, really poor people to attend the upcoming glam opening of the new Miu Miu store in New Bond Street! Like, they can stand outside behind the beautiful big red velvet ropes and watch and cheer and really soak up the glam while mega-stars like Kate Moss, Sophie Dahl and Zoe Ball make their entrances! They'd remember a night like that all their lives, right? And as Noel sez it's about time we all did something to break down the lah-di-dah class barriers in this society and stuff. Respect.

NOEL: We're fookin wild we are. Fookin wild. Like we clocked into a fookin hotel, big swanky fookin place, know what I mean? and Liam, he's like really wound up now, he just goes over to the mini-bar and pulls the door open and swigs back a fookin mini-vodka. And now he's smashed, really smashed and he goes over to the phone and gives it a bit of stick, know what I mean, like he dials all these numbers on it and gets our Mam on the end, just like he owned the fookin place. Then after he'd put the phone down — really put it down on the table provided, like really showin it who's fookin boss — he moves on to the shower. Jeez, what the fook you gonna do with that shower, Liam? I say, but he's so wound up he doesn't fookin listen, he just presses a lever and — whoosh! — all this fookin water splooshes out. Then he grabs the Silvi-fookin-Krin and gives his hair a bit of stick with it and rinses it fookin TWICE! And that's not all. After he's shown the shower who's boss, he grabs the fookin hair-drier and switches it on and blow-fookin-dries his hair like some kinda caged tiger. Christ, Liam, I say — arentcha gonna pick up that towel now? Cos he's left the towel any-fookin-old-how on the floor. Too fookin right I am, mate, he says, and folds it really aggressively and shoves it on the towel-rail. That'll show 'em we're not just a coupla working-class Mancie kids who don't know our fookin manners, says Liam. Too fookin right it will, I say.

MEG: On Boxing Day, we always go for a walk round our 200-acre estate. Noel bought it after the success of the "Shitty Old World in the Ghetto" single back in '96. The grounds include two fully heated swimming pools, one for us, one for the car, three Canova statues (four 'til Liam got up to his tricks with the baseball bat!), two Olympic size personal gymnasiums, his and hers, and a French chateau Noel imported from the Lwarr valley in France. Of course, after 'bout two hundred yards, Noel always gets pissed off with doing our Boxing Day walk, he can't be doing with it, so we say like let's forget it, go back into the house and get our Personal Walkers Jez and Dave to finish it for us while Noel gets someone to order a pizza and stuff. Life's like that.

TREVOR McDONALD

I have just *been* through one of the most extraordinary and *emotionally* draining fortnights of my professional life. But then so has the *whole* country of *which* I am proud to call myself newsreader. *Having* presented News at Ten in its single-anchor *format* for seven (7) years, I have had *to lead* the nation in coming to terms *with* the seismic changes of a News at *Six*-Thirty. It has *been* a fortnight of immense trauma throughout *the* nation, echoing the trauma *undergone* at the death of Diana, Princess *of* Wales. That was news we brought you as *it* happened, with expert *comment* from the full range of those who knew the Princess both well, slightly and not at all. And that's a service we will continue *to* perform in our new time slot.

We calculated *that* six-thirty (6.30) is three and a half (3½) hours earlier than ten (10.00). This *presented* us with an extraordinary challenge. We realised we *would* have to change the much-loved title "News at Ten" to something much *more* appropriate to its time. "News at Seven-Fifteen" had a *note* of urgency to it, but *extensive* audience research told us it might mislead the viewer into *tuning in* three quarters of an hour too late. So after a tremendous amount of soul-*searching*, we hit on "News at Six-Thirty". And it's a title you, the audience, have taken *to your* hearts.

❖

What I think surprised us all was how *much* real emotion was generated by the passing of News at Ten. Everywhere *people* honked their horns. Traffic stopped at red lights and *proceeded* forward on green. Ordinary people in the street came up asking us for *loose* change. Having been inundated by a telephone *call* from a viewer asking for Barry Norman, we were good enough to re-direct her. And after I had entered his cab, a taxi-driver asked me *where* I wanted to go — and then took me straight there. And the response from *our* colleagues in the industry has *been* extraordinarily generous. At the end of our final *programme* on the Friday, our chief executive Stewart Purvis *read* a message from the chairman of ABC News in *New* York. It said, "On Monday your programme will *begin* at six-thirty, and *go on* for another half hour. This is indeed an historic *day* for worldwide news gatherers". And let me assure you of one thing. There weren't *many* dry eyes after that.

❖

Truly **memorable moment (1):** In 1970 our ITN cameraman was first on the scene in Nairobi for the skyscraper *suicide* of a paranoid father-of-two who believed that his every *move* was being watched by film crews. Who would *have* predicted we would come up with a *lead* story to knock that day's Budget from the *headlines*. Our exclusive footage won three prestige *awards* and put ITN *firmly* on the map. Since then, we've covered many skyscraper *plunge* tragedies around the world — but none, I can *safely* say, quite so exciting as that!

❖

News-gathering is a long and arduous *process* at the best of times. But to have three and a half fewer *hours* each day in which to gather it makes for an extraordinary challenge — in *short*, a challenge that is nothing short of extraordinary. Whether it's exclusive footage *of* fresh atrocities in Kosovo, up-to-the-minute flooding in Florida, a rail disaster *causing* tragedy and traffic chaos to millions or the very *latest* from the Paris Fashions, it's our aim to bring it to you in the most accessible and enjoyable *manner*.

❖

At one of the parties last week to *celebrate* the News at Ten years, we talked endlessly about our former colleagues who *made* the programme what it was destined to become, namely News at Ten. Of course everyone remembers Reginald Bosanquet. He was a great character. *Alistair* Burnet will also be long remembered for the great character *he* was. Mike Nicholson was another great *character* who will be long remembered. And it's not likely many *people* will forget Sandy Gall, who was undoubtedly one of the great characters on News at Ten.

Great characters all, who brought *their* great characters to first-class presentation of news *and* current affairs. Many golden moments stand *out* in the memory. I will always remember the time Alistair Burnet showed me a spare tie he always kept in *his* desk, second drawer down "for emergency use only". It was an object *lesson* in the professional approach to live television. And Sandy Gall also taught me a valuable tip that has *lasted* me well down the years. "When presenting the *news*" he told me, "always take care to look straight *at* the camera. If you look in any other *direction*, the viewers may feel you are not *talking* directly to them, but to the wall, or the ceiling". A valuable *tip* from a great character, and one that has lasted me well *down* the years.

❖

Truly memorable *moment* (2): Let no-one tell you we always got *it* right. On 3rd March *1981* News at Ten over-ran by 8 seconds. Result? Red *faces* all round.

❖

By the end of the week we were *looking* back, too, at some of the most memorable events we reported in News at Ten's 32 *years*. We prided ourselves on bringing wars, famines and *natural* disasters, many of them unforgettable, right into the warmth of *your* living-room. This meant that the ordinary fellow in the street *could* feel that he, too, could see people like him dying — and all in prime time, with a commercial *break* in the middle. The style we pioneered gave ITN *journalists* a stake in what we did and gave our *reports* a human dimension. A classic example of that was seen when ITN's *Michael* Nicholson sneezed during a live report from Afghanistan. "Bless you, Michael!" I interjected, *in* a totally unscripted aside. Michael then brought out a *clean* white handkerchief and proceeded to wipe *his* nose. By presenting viewers with the human *dimension* we had brought them immeasurably closer to the very real *conflict* in that war-torn *zone*.

❖

And finally — at 10.30 on that extraordinary *first* evening of Monday 3 July 1967, Alistair Burnet *ended* the very first News at Ten with those historic words, "Tune in tomorrow at *the* same time for some more news". And that's been *our* motto ever since. Thank *you* and *Good* night.

MONTY PYTHON'S FLYING CIRCUS

TERRY JONES: Oooh, hello Mrs Runcible Spoon! It's us! We're back! How's Mrs Codliver Oil today, then?!!!

JOHN CLEESE: Ha ha ha! Classic Python! Seriously though, to me our long-awaited reunion represents a unique opportunity to define our role expectations within the parameters of the giving, ie performing mode, and by so doing to liberate some if not all of our non-positive thoughts and actions from their neo-mechanistic group-pressure preordained behavioural syndromes.

ERIC IDLE: I wish our old mate Graham Chapman was back here, maybe reincarnated as an ice-lolly. Then I could stick him up my arse! Whooops! Classic piece of Pythonesque bad taste there! But Graham would've loved it, bless him! Classic!

TERRY JONES: Spam, spam, spam, spam, spam, spam and spam!!!!!!

ERIC IDLE: Here in LA, I still dine out on that one! Only yesterday, I was talking to Robin Williams — do you know Robin? Lovely guy, incidentally — and he was saying how much he loved all the classic Python stuff — you know, dead parrot, spam, dead parrot, all the classics — and I said, listen, Robin, grab a chair and I'll do one right here! So I ran him through the spam, spam, spam, spam, spam, spam and more spam routine, and he literally fell about. Robin Williams! Beautiful man.

TERRY JONES: Spam, spam, spam, spam, spam, spam and spam!!!

MICHAEL PALIN: I think the reason these sketches are so enduring is that they all have this constant theme, this real unifying philosophy, of wishing to prick the bubble of the pompous, to deflate those who have risen to positions way beyond their talents. Call it thought-provoking, call it irreverent, call it legendary — but what I find totally irresponsible is those critics who just snipe from the sidelines that we are somehow "unfunny" or "over-rated". I mean, how dare they, frankly, how bloody dare they?

TERRY JONES: Oooh! Hello Mrs Cystic Fibrosis! Bad taste joke there! Whoops! Very Pythonesque!

JOHN CLEESE: Great! But seriously, Mike's got a very good point there. I think people who seek to criticise what I'd modestly describe as the Python legend are in some kind of state of denial. But to the extent that as human beings we are all seeking to self-actualise our innermost realities, this very process of opposition to what is, after all, an established and universally accepted set of beliefs — ie, Python as comic legend — may, in itself, represent a healthy outpouring of potentially destructive negativism, a way of coming to terms with the non-positive impulse.

ERIC IDLE: This parrot is dead! This parrot is no more! This parrot is deceased! Polly, polly, polly! Wake up Polly! It's a genuine classic and hard-hitting anti-bourgeois sketch, and one that, here in LA, I'm often regaling my friends with, poolside. Richard Benjamin — do you know Richie? no? smashing bloke — only the other day, Richard Benjamin told me he was truly knocked out by the Dead Parrot sketch, and that he hoped we'd be performing it at our classic upcoming Python reunion. Of course, Richard's got the immortal gift of laughter, too, bless him. Lovely pool, too: kidney-shaped, with beautiful mosaic tiling and underground sauna complex. You really should see it. A real beaut.

TERRY JONES: Spametty spam! Spametty spam-spam! And now for something —

JOHN CLEESE: — completely different! Ha ha! Classic! Of course, this time round we won't deliver an exact reworking of the Spam sketch: that would be absurd, and would simply be playing to the nostalgic impulse within us all instead of upfronting our emotional responses to the present day. Instead, I'm going to input six months into rewriting the classic Spam sketch with a team of three or four fellow writers before playing it to Target Groups across the four main marketing units of the world and then our companies will utilise the feedback to create a globally-enhanced version that will access maximum cultural diversity. Initial Litmus Group reports suggest the word "spam" is itself redundant in usage beyond Britain and parts of North America: our early redrafts of the sketch access the phrase "tinned reconstituted meat product" as an acceptable cross-cultural global alternative.

TERRY JONES: Tinned reconstituted meat product, tinned reconstituted meat product, tinned reconstituted meat product, tinned reconstituted meat product and tinned reconstituted meat product!!! Ooh-err, Mrs Lumbago!

MICHAEL PALIN: Delightfully irreverent in the classic Python tradition — and now universal too! And talking of global, you know, when I go round the world to, say, China (great big country, very, very old, full of truly delightful people) or Australia (vast continent with great big open spaces, where the delightful inhabitants speak English — if you can call it that!!!) I always find that the lovely ordinary people have a superbly Pythonesque sense of humour. You only have to mention the words "Dead Parrot" — and they look at you quite differently!

ERIC IDLE: It's certainly a classic! We had Steve Martin — do you know Steve? lovely man — around the other day, and he was telling me what a terrific influence it was. Hoping to get together with him on a bit of a proj. soon, strictly hush-hush. Have you seen his pool? *Superb.*

TERRY JONES: Oooh! Hello Mrs Stiffy-Corpse! Whoops! Irreverent bad taste! Whoops! Naughty! Naughty! Yes — we're ba-ack! Classic!

BEL MOONEY AT 50

Interestingly, all the babies born — like me — in 1946 will be reaching 50 this year. 1946 was a good crop — Cher, Edwina Currie, Felicity Kendal, Hayley Mills, Sue Lawley, the woman second from the right in the last Dulux ad, you must have seen it, and one of the lunchtime newsreaders on Sky TV. Of this extraordinary list, over half have published books, one has had a string of number one hit records, two have had starring roles in television or on film, and all are household names, except perhaps the last two, who undoubtedly would be if they were better known. Not bad for a single generation, eh? But then my generation have never been frightened of the big questions. Who am I? What am I doing here? To be or not to be? Do you know where you're going to? What's it all about, Alfie? How do you do what you do to me? What's the story, morning glory?

❖

Interestingly, as a generation, I've come to realise we've simply got to let go, we've really got to. But let go of what? I'll tell ya. We've really got to let go of this feeling that we've got to let go. 'Cos to me that's what letting go is really all about.

❖

Interestingly, venturing bravely towards my fiftieth year, never letting a day go by without somehow living through it, crossing this boundary like a thicket in a forest or a thicket to ride, I've gained a unique insight into some of life's deeper mysteries. I have a God-shaped hole in my universe, but what shape is God? To me, he is long and triangular with deep ridges, a bit like a bar of Toblerone, but probably without the nougat. I have a friend, a Christian, who understands my deep longing for God and failure to find him. "Have you looked everywhere?" she asks, imploringly. "What about under the fridge?" When I pray, it is to the Universe, vast and implacable though it is. The Earth itself is my Christ, with the air we breathe the Holy Spirit, the oceans, the major cities and buildings, God the Father, and the smaller things like villages, boats, holiday destinations and home furnishings evenly divided between the Three Kings and the Shepherds.

❖

Interestingly, life is like stumbling into a strange room in the dark. Out of habit, you grope for the light switch, but instead turn on the stereo, waking the dog, which, barking, leaps up and knocks over the china bowl you have just bought for next to nothing at the antiques fair. Unknowingly, you step on a shard of china, yelp, and jump up and down, your shoulder unwittingly rubbing against the light switch causing the light to come on after all. Why don't more people have the courage and vision to see that this is what life is like? Sometimes I worry that we have taught our children so-called "self-expression" but we have not passed on our order and discipline, and there is no logic to their thought.

❖

Interestingly, in my long, long voyage of self-discovery, there's one great lesson I've learnt, and it's this. Do what you did do, don't do what you didn't do. That's just one of the thoughts that came to me in a flash last night, while I was listening to the great Manfred Mann song Doo-Wah Diddy Diddy Dum Diddy Doo. In many deep and unfathomable ways, those classic tracks remain truly inspirational to my generation.

❖

Interestingly, it's a generational thing. For Chrissake, don't get me wrong. We had our faults, my generation, of course we did. We were too optimistic, too generous, too idealistic, too artistic, too full of a whole lotta love we just had to share with everyone, young and old, black and white, rich and poor. Aged seventeen, I had a burning desire to teach the world to sing in perfect harmony and follow through the autumn breeze, oh, peace throughout the land. But look at it another way. My generation was the last not to grow up punch-drunk on television and videos. If we saw an old lady trying to cross the street, we wouldn't mug her and rape her and leave her for dead, we'd light her a joss stick, take her to the top of the building and teach her to fly. My generation didn't go around bombing the Empire State building or creating havoc in supermarkets by poisoning tins of baby food. Instead, there were three things we got our rocks off on: reading and arithmetic. But the younger generation are leaving school firstly iliterate and thirdly inumerate. What we gonna do 'bout it? That's the question. But is it the answer?

❖

Interestingly, it's taken me a full fifty years to discover the humility that seems to me essential to any understanding of my true worth. And suddenly — as I pass my fiftieth birthday, an anniversary that when I was thirty seemed like years away — I have discovered rage. And you know the best advice anyone's every given me? A dear friend took me to one side, turned down the Hendrix on the stereo, put her hands lovingly around my neck and said, "Bel, you must *act your rage*". And I've been following that advice ever since. I rage at the way a single match can act as a flame to a powder keg, drowning it in an ocean of despair. I rage at the way we are turning this planet of ours into a place where several trees must be torn down before the paper can be found to print my passionate message to the planet: please, please, please save our trees. I rage at the way we are denying our old folk their dignity with a patronising blend of condescension, cliche and sentimentality, bless their cotton socks. I rage at the way it takes me two hours to get to the By-Pass Protest group in a journey that should take just half an hour. Where to stop? There's no time to stop. Thirty? Nah — I don't wanna be thirty again. Not with the fire in me now.

❖

Interestingly, I'm a more modest, unassuming and self-doubting person now than I've ever been. It's taken me fifty years, but I've come to realise I'm not the only pebble on the beach: actually, I'm the only sandcastle. But my heart is still young, wild, restless. I'm still crazy after all these years, I still don't want to go to Chelsea and I can't git no na na na na na naaah sat-is-fac-shunn. On balmy summer nights, I sleep beneath the stars in my yurt, happy at 50 that I don't care a fig what other people think. Just so long as they realise I'm truly liberated and liberating, loving and lovely, mild and mellow, super and duper, home and away, cheese and onion, smokey and bacon, still the same old Bel who passionately cares what other people think, bless 'em.

ANDREW NEIL

Good to see you!

Hypocrite of the week: Prince Harry

Prince Harry is a young man born with a silver spoon in his mouth. His family lacked for nothing. Magnificent homes. The finest cars. Ordinary folk waiting on them hand and foot. Expensive foreign jaunts. A toffee-nosed private education. The best meals that money could buy.

And where, you may ask, has that got him?

This week, he was pictured by a leading newspaper walking along with a shoelace undone. Completely and utterly undone.

So where's the pomp and ceremony in that, eh?

Harryshoelacegate is destined to be seen as one of the most shameful episodes in the history of our Royal Family.

Once they were the pride of the nation. Now they are a family of scruffs, too damn lazy even to keep their shoelaces properly tied.

And who's interested in them any more, anyway?

Not me, and that's for sure. Like most ordinary folk, I have better things to do with my time than worry about whether Prince Harry's shoe-lace is done up or not.

And it's about time the self-deluding younger Royals recognised this fact.

❖

Life in the 1980s was a rollercoaster ride — but I wasn't scared to ruffle Establishment feathers. On The Sunday Times, I broke many scoops of which I have every right to be proud, and no one can tell me I can't, or they'll find out what it is to cross swords with Andrew Neil —

• In 1983, we revealed that HRH Princess Margaret was a high-level Soviet plant with a secret mission to destroy our democratic government. They say her career never recovered.

• In 1985, we scooped the world to reveal that Sky Television was now the number one rated television station in the world — a view reinforced by a private poll of our formidable team of top-ranking News International executives.

• In 1986, we exclusively serialised the Secret Diaries of the Loch Ness Monster — thus putting paid to a Government cover-up that had denied the existence of this monster at the very heart of the Establishment for nearly 100 years.

• In 1988, we revealed that TV supremo Des O'Connor was tipped for the top job in British Nuclear Electric. My hard-hitting editorial spelt it out: "To appoint a superannuated television crooner to the top job in nuclear energy is nothing short of madness," I wrote. My words must have struck at the very heart of Establishment decision-making.

Sure enough, no more was ever heard of the matter again. They say his career never recovered.

I achieved all this — and more — because I had no time for the pathetic blandishments and baubles of a decadent English Establishment. As Mr Murdoch himself said at an exclusive dinner-party given in my honour in a luxury private suite in the top-ranking Dorchester Hotel, attended by many senior Government ministers and high-powered media commentators: "Neil — you have no need for fol-de-rols. You've shown us all the true meaning of editorial independence. You've always fought tooth and nail for your right to say exactly what I think — and my god I respect you for it!"

Bold words, indeed — but life at the Court of the Sun King was not always plain sailing. Those who survive a decade at Rupert's court have to be totally loyal to their master, kow-towing to his every whim. Not me. For ten years, whenever he entered the room, I made a point of standing up to the man. "Be seated," he would eventually say. But I would insist on my absolute right as editor to remain on my knees, pursuing my own agenda. In retrospect, perhaps I was too keen to assert my independence, but I always made a display of unbuckling his trousers and spending a reasonable measure of my own time independently licking away at the behind of this Jekyll-and-Hyde character with my rough and gritty anti-Establishment tongue.

But over the years Rupert was to become increasingly jealous of my power. Colleagues informed me he was green with envy at the way I singlehandedly brought down the Berlin Wall and sick to the gills that I had been able to appoint the next President of the USA in a hard-hitting Sunday Times editorial. I daresay he was also bitterly jealous of my skiing activities, and of my well-publicised success

with the lovely ladies in my life. We were at daggers drawn
— but it was a battle Rupert could never hope to win. You
see, by this time I had established myself an effective
alternative power-base as presenter of one of London's most
influential early morning radio phone-in programmes; it was
from here that I was to plot Rupert's overthrow. Eventually
things came to a head. "You're fired!" he said. He had
walked straight into my trap.

A year before, I had secretly invested in a John Bull
Printing Outfit, complete with every letter of the alphabet. I
was thus able to write, print and publish my very own
miniature Sunday Times, week in, week out, from my own
power-base on the kitchen table. It has been going nearly
three years now. I can assure you it has the toffee-nosed
English Establishment running scared. They're terrified that
one day it'll find its way on to the news-stands — and then
they'll have to beg for mercy. And what does Rupert
Murdoch, the Sun King himself, think of my new power?
The guy's so terrified, he hasn't mentioned me to a living
soul in three years.

And some say his career has never recovered.

Good to see you!

ADAM PHILLIPS' MONOTONY

1.

Monotony is unexpected, bold, tantalising. There are so
many different kinds of monotony, depending on the type
of person one is — a person who prefers talking about roads
or a person who prefers talking about the weather — that
monotony is perversely erotic.

2.

Too many cooks spoil the broth. The broth is spoilt by too
many cooks. The paragraph gets bigger with the sentences
one places in it. The more sentences one places in it, the
bigger the paragraph gets.

But perhaps, after all, the broth always wanted to be
spoilt, so as to attract too many cooks?

3.

The separation of the word Monotony into two equal halves — Mono and Tony — begs the question: who's Tony?

Is Tony a single man who pops in from time to time to help with the garden? Or the name of the local fishmonger? Or is he something more than that — a dyadic, a schephelomenon, even a Weltanschauung? Who knows? Without his Mono, Tony — toe, knee — would lack the full body of monotony.

4.

There are two kinds of modern thinker — the thinker who thinks it clever to divide everything into two kinds (two kinds of thinker, two kinds of teabag, two kinds of monotony) and the thinker who prefers flip paradox (Q. When is a paradox not a paradox? A. Now.). I belong to the second kind, the one which doesn't divide everything into two kinds. Or, paradoxically, I would belong to it, if I did. And so you are left wondering: is there no depth to which this man will not think?

5.

To grow more monotonous, or to struggle against it? There is always something to resist, something to defy. The fascinating are the same as the monotonous: they drive the same cars, their favourite colour is pale green and they call their daughters Sally. Monotony is like cabbages, only spelt differently, and with another meaning.

6.

Death is a necessary ingredient of monotony. In fact, death is a necessary ingredient of so many apercus. The inclusion of death adds grandeur to even the most obvious thought. For monotony by its nature goes on for a long time: like death.

7.

In future, everyone will be monotonous for fifteen minutes. I monotonise, therefore I am.

8.

Monotony makes the heart grow fonder. Most people would not be monotonous if they had not heard monotony spoken of.

9.

Monotony makes the world go round. Monotony, monotony, monotony, that would be fonotony, it's a rich man's world.

10.

Repetition is the memory of repetition. But, on the other hand, repetition is the memory of repetition.

11.

What is the answer? What was the question? What are we doing here? Why are you reading this? Why am I writing it? Questions, questions, questions. At the beginning of a love affair, you ask, "Has there ever been a smile so beautiful, lips so warm and loving?" At the end of a love affair, you ask, "Isn't it about time you learnt to pick your own bloody socks up off the floor?" In a nutshell, this is what disfoundationalistic versionality-based progress narratives are all about. The questions might change, but the monotony remains.

12.

Proust, Eliot, Lacan, Freud, Shakespeare, Klein, Plath, Donne, Jung, Phillips. They all have one thing in common: they are all mentioned here, in section 12 of "Monotony".

13.

Around the ragged rock, the ragged rascal ran. No. Around the ragged rock, the profoundly ragged rascal ran. No. From a psychoanalytic point of view, around the parallel text of the ragged rock, the profoundly ragged rascal ran, strangely — perversely — disillusioned by the secular religion of monotony.

Yes, that's better.

14.

Just as there are only two kinds of weather — hot and cold — so there are only two kinds of monotony — very monotonous monotony, and not-quite-so monotonous monotony. All monotony is by its very nature monotonous: but no monotony is more monotonous than my monotony: which is what makes it so monotonous.

So there is an end to monotony. Or is the end just another beginning?

HAROLD PINTER

Shit.
That's not a word you're comfortable with?
You're not comfortable with that word?
You're not comfortable with that shit?
Well I don't give a shit.
So shit, shit, shit, shit.
And shit.

I wrote the above poem, which I called "Shit", while being driven in my courtesy limousine from Heathrow to Campden Square. Such was my fury that I had completed a final draft before we had left the airport precincts. I later re-titled the poem "Utter Shit", giving it extra force.

Recognising it at once as a very important piece of work, I

biked it round to the editor of The Observer for immediate publication.

In that Sunday's Observer: nothing.

In the next Sunday's Observer: nothing.

I got put through to the editor: "Oh dear, Harold," he said. "It's obviously a very striking poem but..."

"Don't 'Oh dear, Harold' me, chum. I thought you were a serious newspaper," I said. "Can't you see it's about what the Americans are doing? If you don't print it, the war will continue and you'll have blood on your hands. It's up to you, chum."

At this point, my wife, Lady Antonia, came in bearing a plate of fairy cakes. I took one and stuffed it into my mouth. Then another. Then another. And another. I like fairy cakes. Fairy cakes are what I like.

"Personally, I love the poem, Harold, but I feel our readers might not..." said the editor.

At this point, I exploded. Fairy cake shot out of my mouth like a hundred bombs from a nuclear arsenal, hitting random civilian targets — the smoked-glass coffee-table, the porcelain figures on the mantelpiece, the carriage clock, the sleeping Pekinese, Antonia's new frock, clean on that morning — without a thought for human life.

❖

The next day, I wrote an open letter to the Prime Minister of this country:

"Dear Mr Blair, I enclose a copy of my most recent poem. It is 'Utter Shit'. I believe that, if we are to divert a disaster, you should give it sober thought.

It was written to express my feelings of revulsion at the way the Americans are blowing the shit out of Kosovo and fucking it up the arse before wiping their noses with the soiled toilet paper and tossing it on the ground to be sniffed over by dogs. A more mature attitude is needed.

My wife, Lady Antonia, and I agree that this is a situation which cannot be allowed to go on. The US elephant must be stopped. It has trumpeted too long, keeping its neighbours up at night. First we must shoot it. Dead. Then we must cut off its tusks. With wire wool, we must then grind those tusks down. So we can sell the powder as an aphrodisiac to underprivileged nations. Then they can fuck the dead corpse of America just like America fucked the shit out of them. I believe this to be the only feasible solution to the appalling state of affairs developing in Eastern Europe at the present time."

❖

No reply. Just the usual piss — The Prime Minister thanks you for your "Utter Shit", was interested to hear your etcetera etcetera.

But it didn't end there. The next day, a man in his forties appeared at the door. In uniform. Said he'd come to read the meter.

"What meter? We don't have any meter," I said, barring his way. I experienced an overwhelming urge to wrestle him to the ground and spit my spittiest spit in his face.

"Yes we do, darling. The electricity meter, just outside the servants' sitting-room in the basement," said my wife, Lady Antonia. She was wearing a fresh frock, clean on.

"You'd better come in then," I said. I wanted to smack him in the bollocks. Hard.

Something about the man alerted me that he was actually a senior Cabinet minister. I knew instinctively that he had been sent by the Blair regime at Downing Street to flush me out. I was a dissident. "They want to flush dissidents down the toilet," I whispered to Antonia.

Antonia agreed. "Lavatory," she said.

❖

"All done," said the man in his forties.
"Now clear bloody off," I said.

"Harold says thank you so much for coming," repeated Antonia. "I'll show you out."

"Yes," I said, "Antonia will show you the bloody door, matey. And tell your chums in Downing Street that I'm not going to take it up the arse any longer."

The next day, I read that they had dropped another lot of bombs on Belgrade. The present regime must have thought it would teach me a lesson. Well, you've got another think coming, Mr Tony Bloody Blair. You can send a meter man round and attach electrical cables to my genitals whenever you like, but you're still not going to silence me, chum.

❖

Some time later, a man calls. He represents himself as a postman. Cap, uniform, the lot. He has an electricity bill. They want to charge us for our electricity. The same electricity that goes into making those planes that have fucked the shit out of Belgrade. Now they are trying to force us to pay for their crap. Antonia and I are dissidents — dissi-bloody-dents — in our own land. Next they'll lock a ball and chains round Antonia's ankles and gag her so that she won't be able to read an extract from her latest work, "Dearest Darling Duchesses: A Social History" at the Waterstone's wine-and-cheese evening. Bastards.

And all because they were so shit-scared by my latest poem. In a rage, I write to The Guardian:

"Sir: US foreign policy can be defined as follows: 'Kiss my arse or I'll kick your head in.' Their level of intelligence is infantile. And Clinton is the shittiest shit who ever shat shit."

And they print it. That's the way they stifle dissent in this country. They print what you write. But it won't work, Tony, old chum. Not while I'm alive to arm-wrestle you to the ground and suffocate you with my bare fist, it won't.

Yours ever, Harold.

PS. Lady Antonia sends her regards.

MICHAEL PORTILLO

It was a truly terrible night for the Conservatives. Truly terrible. But something happened to me on that truly terrible night, something unexpected and slightly shocking and really rather wonderful.

I became a different person.

I stopped listening to Wagner. Now I listen to the more caring rhythms of Roger Whittaker.

I put aside my Spengler and my Nietzsche. These days, I prefer the more compassionate vision of Catherine Cookson.

I no longer wear dark pin-striped suits and stiff collars with flashy ties. Instead, I go for a softer look: pastel shades of mauve and cerise, with fabrics gentle to the touch — preferably cashmere if I can afford it!

The day after that truly terrible night, I gave up eating steak. Today, I always make a bee-line for the Vegetarian menu. Carrots, gently shredded, are a particular favourite. Cucumber, beetroot, apples, bran — lovely. Just so long as there's no animal killed on my behalf. Animals deserve better than that.

Mike Portillo: Peter, you're a risk-taker.

Peter Mandelson: So are you, Mike. We don't mind sticking up for our beliefs, do we?

Mike Portillo: And what's more you're a genuinely lovely, lovely guy.

Peter Mandelson: Mike — you've changed your hair, right? To me, it shows the softer, more gentle you. The side of you the public never gets to see.

Mike Portillo: Thanks, Peter. And you've lost weight. Hey, you're looking great!

Peter Mandelson: Sorry you lost that seat, Mike. Can't wait to see you bounce back!

Mike Portillo: Bless you for that, Peter. Must dash! Ciao!

❖

And as you see, I don't talk any more. I prefer to listen.

Yes, I now spend hours and hours every day of the week travelling up and down the country, listening to ordinary, decent people telling me exactly why they loathe my guts. Then I disappear behind the door for a short while. Blow my nose. Wipe away those tears. Take a deep breath.

And then I go back and ask them to tell me again.

Mike Portillo: Ordinary person, I'd really like to know exactly what you think is wrong with me.

Ordinary person: You're arrogant. You're cruel. You're selfish. You're out of touch. And not only that. You smell.

Mike Portillo: It's very good of you to tell me that. And would you say, on reflection, that I am also heartless and snooty and too big for my boots?

Ordinary person: Certainly. And you make little children cry, you horrid man.

Mike Portillo: Thank you, thank you. I'm so terribly, terribly sorry. I want to apologise to you and all the other ordinary persons up and down the country for what we as a Party did to you. For these and all the sins I cannot remember, I am truly sorry.

❖

Well, that ordinary person was clearly very upset by the way we Tories ran the country. Pretty depressing news for us there, I'm afraid. But I've listened, and I've learnt. And if that ordinary person had one message for us, I think it was this. Stick to your guns. You're doing a great job. This lot in New Labour have got nothing new to offer. Carry on just the same as before, and you'll walk it.

A sobering message, and one we must heed. But a message not entirely without hope. Because basically what the ordinary people of this country are telling me loud and clear is this. Yes, we made one or two mistakes in presentation. Yes, we probably spent too much time trying to sort out the affairs of the country, and not enough time buttering up the broadcasters. And yes, we had a bit of trouble getting our message over. But basically they like us and respect us and they can't wait for us to get rid of this Labour government.

Mike Portillo: William, I know you to be a man of intelligence, conviction, charm, good looks, humour and an outstanding fashion sense. But the ordinary people think the opposite. They think you're stupid, out of touch, pompous, ugly and cold-hearted — in short, a complete and utter prat. What are you going to do about it?

William Hague: We've got to build on that perception. We've got to reach out to all those people and say, hey, yes, I may be a prat — but at least I'm a complete and utter prat. We've got to show them we're undergoing a total transformation. And that with their help, I'll become an even more thorough-going prat in the years ahead.

❖

And the listening process continues. The way I listen is to keep my mouth closed and stare in the direction of the other person. When their lips seem to have stopped going up and down, I shake their hand and say, "Thank you — *insert first name* — for letting me share your opinions. Goodbye *insert first name*!"

Yes, it's good to listen. It's certainly made me a much more caring, thoughtful person. Today, I'm wearing a casual shirt with V neck jersey and brown slacks. Tomorrow, I'm planning to read the new Maeve Binchy in a spotty cravat.

Yesterday I had this frank exchange with an old man in a dole queue:

Me: You must be Albert! Great!

Old Man: I've been out of a job and homeless for twelve years and I hate your bloody guts.

Me: Super. Super. And what do you think of me, Albert?

Old Man: Fuckin bastard.

Me: That's the spirit, Albert! And any special message for the Conservatives?

Old Man: Piss off the bloody lot of you.

Me: Super! Lovely! It's been great to listen! Lots of fun!

On reflection, I think what Albert is saying is that we in the Conservative party will have his vote if we sharpen up our opposition to the single currency. And so begins the process of rebuilding trust in the community — by listening. By the way, have you heard the new Chris de Burgh? Mmmm. It's as warm as a drop of dew on a mellow Autumn day. Ciao!

ROGER SCRUTON

In a modern world where everything is for sale, where value is price and price is value, where cushions are everywhere and electric "cookers" are preferred to camp-fires, where pop-singers moan "Yeah Yeah Yeah Sex Yeah Yeah More Sex" and are rewarded for their screeches with the transient passions of teenaged girls, where petticoats are scorned and bowler-hats considered old-fashioned, where adolescents "snog" each other after a moment's acquaintance on "bean-bags" in the corners of poorly-lit "discotheques", where pampered patients insist on wishy-washy "anaesthetics" before undergoing major operations, where unkempt youths are permitted to plunge their tongues headlong into the cleavages of pert young sluts without a "please" or a "thank you", where drugs, alcohol and all types of sexual activity, performed at every angle, endlessly divert the youngster from his studies, where 26 year old former nude model Miss Geri Halliwell need only don the tightest and shortest of dresses and parade about stage flaunting her bountiful bust and wiggling her buttocks in a shameless and provocative fashion in order to divert Professors from their readings of Goethe and Nietzsche, in this world there are no longer standards, either aesthetic or moral, that continue to hold force, as our culture spins helplessly towards oblivion. And Sporty Spice, with her new longer hairdo, devilishly bared arms, clingier trouser and flirtatious glint — suggestive, rapacious, unquenchable, undeniable — must also bear the brunt of the blame for the downfall of Western civilisation.

❖

Whatever happened to faulty electrical fittings? In the old days, two or three youngsters would be electrocuted every day through haphazard wirings. But no more. Verily, things do not always change for the better, I fear.

❖

There is no animal I would rather ride on an English hunt than a horse. The donkey is too stubborn, the camel too slow, the duck too flighty. I once rode to hounds upon the back of a chihuahua, but we had not leapt the first fence before the wretched beast perished beneath me, thoughtlessly leaving me to wrap it round my neck as an effective headscarf and to leap the fence all by myself.

Verily, the English horse is a creature of strength and beauty unsurpassed. I believe, moreover, that I shalst ne'er forget the first occasion upon which I found cause to ascend my doughty steed. Seventeen-hand horses were snorting and heaving to every side, their buttocks rippling with muscles like the seething wakes of ocean liners. Dobbin's neck was arched, his head down, with the bit held firmly in his teeth;

his feet were dancing on the road, his tail swishing provocatively to and fro, and great surges of life rose through his quarters, invading and inflaming me on their way to his heart and to his head.

Ah, most equine of steeds! A novice, I climbed into the saddle and from this great height looked out o'er the clear view of yonder English hills. A crack of the whip, a crick of the spur, and Dobbin was up and away, like yesteryear's winged Perseus flying o'er lofty Mount Olympus! Never had I felt such a sensation, for I was now travelling backwards at great gallop, the swish-swish-swish of Dobbin's mighty tail beating heavily into my visage. But where was his head? Through the hairs of his tail, I searched for it. Did not every mare perforce need a head? It was at this point I realised I had ascended my mount with a degree of incorrectitude, and I was facing the rear.

Civilisation continues through adherence to established codes. I did not intend to discommode the hunt by calling my horse to a halt and turning around in my saddle. Instead, I employed Dobbin's tail as reins, turned my helmet around and urged my noble steed to proceed backwards, thus maintaining my dignity at no cost to my fellow horsemen.

❖

Whatever happened to good old tuberculosis? It was a disease of great character, perfectly adapted to these ancient isles. But now — despite many broken promises of a revival — it has all but petered out. In a modern world fixated with witless health, TB is sorely missed.

❖

Being unpopular is never easy; but being unpopular in a good cause is a shield against despair. It was never easy, amidst the lax standards of the 1970s, to lend my voice to demands for stiff custodial sentences to be meted out to all children caught chewing bubblegum. It was not easy, in the liberal ethos of universities in the 1960s, to campaign for a statue of General Franco to be erected outside the Students Union at the University of Essex. Nor is it easy now, in the Blairite nineties, to speak up for that small but fiercely independent-minded minority who wish to apply electric shock treatment to all senior citizens who prove persistently late in paying their electricity bills. But I gain succour for my courage from those ancient English souls — Shakespeare, Wordsworth, Johnson, Chaucer, Churchill, Powell — who have verily entrusted me with their deep-seated beliefs in our ancestral freedoms. If this requires me to court unpopularity, so be it. As yellow sunlight pours over the English countryside and the blue-grey clouds in the distance scud hither and thither, uncorrupted, pliable, folding and forming in obedience to the will of God, I shall ne'er cease from campaigning for higher taxes on nurses and firemen, the selling of all British lifeboats to foreign powers for use as tools of indiscriminate homicide, and the renaming of all Mandela Streets throughout our land to something more in keeping with our native tradition, such as Enoch Avenue. Meanwhile, the gap left at the top of the Liberal Democratic Party must be filled by a man of proven grit, stamina and direction. Step forward, Augusto Pinochet — but don't expect it to make you popular.

❖

Whatever happened to dogs that viciously bit postmen leaving them grievously wounded, perhaps mortally so? English dogs now lack the vim and spirit to do anything but sit, scamper, or wag their tails. These days, I fear even the dogs have gone to the dogs.

W.G. SEBALD

It had grown uncommonly dark and sultry, the clouds painfully laden as though ready to sear the earth once more with their translucent acid, when I set out on my Summer holidays. Holidays! The word itself, a stifled and tortuous amalgam of "holly", that fiercest and most spiteful of all trees, with its sharp, shiny, pox-green edges ready to strike out and pierce human skin, causing blood, a dark reddish-grey, greyish-red, to drop out, willy-nilly, onto the earth below, staining the soil in perpetuity, and "days", with its dull echo of daze, in which I so often find myself after finishing these sentences, some of them as long and distracted as those sentences handed out with unnerving efficiency by the Guatemalan Lord Chief Justice to the Netherlandish invaders of the Indonesian island of Iwu-Miju in 1473, after the Brecon uprising commemorated in the poem by Swinburne after he had taken a cup of tea — a cup fatally calamitous for two pure-white sugar lumps, who can have known little of their destruction but for those few dreadful seconds when they experienced the unsettling feeling, common to all human civilisation, of being dropped into hot, brown liquid with an abrupt flick of the wrist, there to disintegrate into nothingness, never to return — the entire and dreadful word, "holidays", forcing one to attempt to suppress a mounting sense of dizziness in the face of looming catastrophe.

❖

It was a dark, overcast day when I arrived on the beach with my bucket and spade, or it would have been if the sun had not been blazing down on me, as though spurred in its hatred by some half-remembered vendetta, unforgiving in its burning, hell-like cruelty. My feet seemed to blister in despair and to scream out in silent agony as the sand slithered and slimed its way, viper-like, into their mis-shapen crevices, holes between limbs, all worn away by the ravages of time. What could I build with my spade and my bucket, the two of them working in unison, that might hope to endure longer than a single tide? I strode despairingly along the beach, taking note of what others had constructed. Sandcastles! But to me the idea of erecting a castle of sand was out of the question if there was no cement-mixer to hand. I hesitated no more, immediately walking, all alone with my bucket and spade, to a distant builders' merchants in the outer reaches, terrifyingly isolated, of the locality. "I will be immediately needing a cement mixer for the construction of a beach-castle" I told the merchant, "You may be assured I shall be providing my own sand and water." He looked at me with the bemused expression I have observed before on those startled to find a stranger among them, however proficient he may be in the language of English. There was no time to lose: I soon found myself back at the same stretch of beach, pulling my cement-mixer behind me, the grains of sand, like so many tiny eyeballs, staring in mute hatred at me as I prepared to turn them to stone.

❖

The sky appeared blue, but I knew that, somewhere else in the world, yet more clouds, black and bruised, were gathering. Immediately above me, a seagull swooped, its wings stretched fully out, as though an unseen torturer were pulling them to breaking-point until they disclosed their secret. But what secret does the seagull hold? This one conducted its incessant squawking with an earnest intensity, yet its almost bird-like language meant nothing at all. Whenever one cuts in half a seagull that has been killed with ethyl alcohol one is struck by how utterly useless it now looks, each half unable to flap in even the most basic manner. Anton Chekhov must have known this distinctive, bewildering feature about seagulls when he wrote his play *The Cherry Orchard*, for almost exactly three years and two months earlier and only six hundred and forty seven miles away, a Prussian fisherman with pale brown hair had finally assembled the largest collection of ostrich eggs under a single roof. Ten years on, due to faulty sand-based cement in the fixtures, the roof was to crumble, and the entire collection was to lie in smithereens. High above me in the air, the gull continued upon its vacuous and erratic journey through a sky still glowering in fury at the ceaseless intrusion of the crazed sun.

❖

The sky loomed over me like a bright blue package containing heavy objects about to fall on the world from a great height. "Strawberry or Orange, mate?" said the man. I had asked for an ice-lolly and now the salesman in the van was cross-questioning me as to my exact meaning. "A Mivvi" I replied. "I know that, mate" he responded, curtly, "But Strawberry or Orange?" It was then that I remembered that Orange is the colour of the robes that adorn the corpses of women in Delhi who have died hideous deaths, a haunting and melancholy detail I have never been able to shed from my memory when ordering a lolly. "Orange, please" I said mournfully. The Mivvi, I was later to discover, is named after Dr Hans Mivvi of Zurich, the eighteenth-century apothecary whose Almanac de Mivvi, first published in Rome in 1781 — the very same year that a 92 year old woman was burnt as a witch in Bury St Edmunds — pioneered the notion of an iced comestible wrapped around another iced comestible, the two of them then placed on a stick. Yet the Mivvi ice-lolly has always seemed to me god-forsaken in its bewildered iciness, an iciness brought into savage relief by the plaintive flavouring of its outer lollyhood, so that the insertion of the Mivvi into the mouth induces a terrifying sense of déjà-vu in the hapless consumer, as though mankind itself were frozen for those few minutes on a stick, to be placed into the mouth of nothingness until it melts, the sole memento of our existence a few fast-fading orange drips on the chin of oblivion. With the sun setting behind me, reminding me of a bad egg thrown haphazardly into a darkening bin, I end my first day on the sodden beach. On this very day three hundred and ninety seven years ago, something unspeakingly dreadful happened. But what? I spot a congealed chip on the worn beach, pick it up, suck on it, and struggle to remember.

FRANK & NANCY
SINATRA

NANCY: His complexities run deep, so very deep. My Dad, Francis Albert Sinatra, is a man who embraces consistency yet embodies contradictions. A man who is so deep that he's almost shallow, yet so broad that he's almost narrow. A man who will stand up for the little guy, just so long as that little guy stands up for him whenever he enters the room. A man who dines with Presidents, yet never forgets the name of any ordinary two-bit motherfucker who tries to mess with him. A man who is an all-American hero and a legend, yet a patriot who'll cross the road to open a gaming casino so the honest Joes of this great nation can do something useful with their hard-earned dimes. Love ya, Daddy.

FRANK: Love you too, chicken. A thought. The world we live in can be a cruel, lonely place for people like us. People who dare to sing and to dance. People who defy the system by reaching out to the hearts of others to whisper "I Love You". I say this with sadness, but we will always be feared and despised by those uptight, locked-in little people who are bewildered by the rare and magical secrets we possess. But, still, we must extend our arms around those poor, persecuted souls. And we must clutch them tight. And tighter. And still tighter. *Tighter still I said*. Until they begin to confess that there may be value in a songsmith. And enchantment in this legendary lover of his fellow man.

NANCY: Dad — you say such beautiful things. You are a running river flowing into a glacier of burnished gold, a sea-trout flying on silken wings up, up, up to the highest valley of them all. You know something? One day when I was a little girl of, say, five or six years of age, I was running along the patio and I fell over and cut my knee. And I hollered and screamed and screamed and hollered. And I'll never forget your face that day, Dad. It remained so serene, so calm, with such deep inner tranquillity that you remained untroubled by outside events, seeing them as necessary to progress in the great tide of man. And that taught me a lesson I'll never forget, not in all the years God allows me to remain on this beautiful planet we call America. And that lesson is this. No man — no woman either — should ever go any place without a pair of top-of-the-range earplugs.

And then, Dad, you did something I'll remember all my days. After just twenty short minutes, you looked in my direction, across to the crumpled little girl splattered on the patio, tears flooding her dimples, and then you looked back at your close friend Johnny "The Skunk" Debrazzo. And in your softest, warmest, sweetest voice, you whispered: "Find the guy who laid those paving-stones and tell him Frankie says he don't exist no more."

I think it's the artist in you, Dad. You're a force of nature that demands respect, a tidal wave of love and compassion washing away all those who stand in its wake.

FRANK: You know, chicken, I think it's my honesty that frightens and devastates people. They aren't used to dealing with true sincerity. My songs reach into the very heart of mankind — classics like "Whoopsy, Doopsy, There Goes My Boopsy", "There's a Song in My Heart and a Drip in My Hat" and "I like a Girl Who Darns and Knits".

Way back, I threw a party in my honor to celebrate my Humanitarian of the Year Award from The Las Vegas Chamber of the Frank Sinatra Appreciation Society of which I had the honor to be Life President. As the world knows, it's a charitable venture. We ask for just a few dollars a week from non-members; in return we promise them and their families total security to pursue the great American dream.

But who the hell was going to present me with this honor? We needed a guy with a reputation for probity, straight-dealing and sheer big-heartedness. A guy whose friendships with important people, including Presidents of the United States, a guy whose numerous well-attested acts of private charity would make him a suitable recipient of the honor of making the presentation to Ol' Blue Eyes here. So I thought of all the good friends I've been blessed with down the years. Richard M. Nixon? A great President, but a great President with a perspiration problem. Dean Martin? One helluva guy and helluva opening act. But let's not confuse statures. I hate to see a guy look small. Bing? Sammy? Perry? Legends, yes, but only legends in their own lifetimes. Nope. There was only one guy, one all-American legend we felt we could approach to make this historic presentation. Yes, Ol' Blue Eyes himself, Mister Francis Albert Sinatra.

I accepted the responsibility warmly and with compassion. When it came to the presentation, I shook hands with myself in a way that conveyed my appreciation of all I had done to make America the country it is today. "Frank," I said. "We need more legends like you."

In response I looked a teensy bit bashful and — well — kinda modest. "Coming from you, Frank, that's really something," I replied, tears in my eyes. An unforgettable moment for everyone present — just me and the great Frank. Frank and the great me.

NANCY: I want to clear up one thing about my father forever, okay? He never met Fatso "The Pony" Gymkhana or the ice-cream giant Mr Toni "The Chisel" Softee, other than once or twice when he may have bumped into them by chance on his yacht or at a christening or some such family reunion. Notwithstanding these chance meetings — not more than eleven or twelve a year, and never lasting longer than a month at a time — Frank Sinatra never had any contact whatsowhomwhichsoever with any members of any organisation of any type anywhere in the world. He's spent a lifetime denying these persistent untruths by refusing to dignify them with a response. Nor did he ever instruct his attorneys to punch firmly on the nose any son of a bitch who continued to bleat those doggone lies before giving him a smart kick in the groin and leaving him in the gutter where he belongs. And anyone who says he did is a dead man.

FRANK: A beautiful tribute, chicken, really beautiful. Like all my family — Tina, Frankie and all my beautiful wives — you've taken Frank's advice, you've lived a life that's full, you've followed me over each and every highway. But more, much more than this — you did it My Way.

THE SPICE GIRLS

Welcome to GIRL POWER! This is the only column that's written by ALL OF US especially for ALL OF YOU! And it's the only place you'll find out exactly what us SPICE GIRLS are really, really like — and you know that anything we do for you is always totally honest, totally happening and 100% PURE SPICE!

EMMA: To me, GIRL POWER means if Mel C wants to wear trakkie bottoms, why the hell shouldn't she? Girl Power's about TAKING CONTROL OF YOUR LIFE and doing not what other people want you to do but what other people don't not want you not to do, but not if that's not what you don't want to do and definitely not if what you want to do is not what they want you not to do. It's that simple, girls!

MEL B: I'm a bit of a nutter, me. You'll never get me conforming. Not bloody likely. I thrive on chaos and being spur-of-the-moment. Like, last week I just felt like half a shandy from the hotel mini-bar. I just didn't care if it did my head in. The others said don't. But what did I do? I only went ahead and did it, didn't I? And to me that's GIRL POWER.

MEL C: GIRL POWER means there's a lot more to our music than most of the pop stuff we get lumped with. A lot of groups are just writing what they think the public will want, like what's going to sell. But we're not into that, no way. We write what we want to write, right? Our songs have INNER MEANING. Like:

I wanna, I wanna, I wanna, I wanna
I wanna want my wanna wants
And what you want I wanna want
I wanna I wanna I wanna want want

That's all about the way you sometimes want something, and sometimes you can have it, which is wicked, and sometimes you can't, which is crappy bollox. Basically, it's a Buddhist song. I'm into Buddha. Like, I gotta tattoo of the guy on my left buttock. But I don't fancy him. No way. Crikey. I hate guys who are ALL HANDS.

GERI: GIRL POWER? It's about taking control of your own dynasty. We're all feminists, and we've given feminism A KICK UP THE ARSE, 'cos what we say is you can THINK POLITICAL even when you're got up in a boob-tube and thigh-length boots. Which international politician would I most like to snog? Nelson Mandela. He's not just really smiley and snoggable but he's also a guy who knows what he really, really wants — and is prepared to spend his life on telly just to get it!

VICTORIA: GIRL POWER is all about being what you are. Like, I'm Posh Spice, and they all call me that 'cos I talk posh and I think posh and I act posh and I don't give a toss. If I want to get drunk or eat lots of cream cake then I do. We want young girls at school to relate to us, to be one of us. Kids can smell bullshit a mile off, it smells like... bullshit.

GERI: I sang 'If you put two and two together, you see what friendship is for'. I immediately saw the 2 plus 2 = 4 pun in that. I tried to explain it to the others. But they didn't get it. I got a C in Sums, you know. I'm always getting Sums into our songs, just to make them more brainy. See if you can spot the sums in this one:

I wanna be 3 2 live my life
I really 8 being no 1
Come and 5 with me
4 as long as I'm yours and you are 9

MEL B: We're all deep thinkers, like, really really deep, four foot six inches deep, easy, maybe even five. So a song like

I wanna show you my tits
But I can't undo my bra-a
I wanna go all the way
Or anyway reasonably fa-ar

you can take on a lot of different levels, like level 1 or level 2 or level 3, depending where you're at and where you're goin'.

EMMA: With our talent we aim to give every single person we come into contact with a zest for life. We broaden their minds, and make them aware of the real world outside. That's what I call GIRL POWER. So, like, the girl who's stuck working in a factory all hours can hear us sing

My fave poet's Seamus Heaney
An' I'm gonna buy a Lamborghini

and she can think, like, 'Wow, yeah; right — that's MY LIFE too — and it's really great The Spice Girls are living it for me!'

VICTORIA: Don't let no one tell you it's not hard work 'cos it is. Some days when we're doing videos we have to mime our hearts out for hours and we have to look good too if the body doubles aren't available. And the press! We've had to really gen up on politics, I can tell you! Me? I vote Liberals. Wicked Jeremy Thorpe lights my fire, and I reckon he's just the guy to take this country kicking and screaming into the 20th century. GIRL POWER — it's all about unity and solidarity between nations — and everyone else can just piss off.

❖

So what's GIRL POWER? GIRL POWER is when:
• You and your mates reply to wolf whistles by shouting "Get your arse out!"
• You put on your WONDERBRA and start THINKING TOTALLY SPIRICHOO about heavy things like how to FIND GOD and how to get Inner Peace and where to get your hands on Top Shop's Summer Collection.
• You show you couldn't give a monkey's for WHAT MEN THINK OF YOU SEXUALLY. Instead, you PUT ON THE LIPSTICK, THRUST OUT YOUR TITS and STRUT YOUR STUFF — just the way YOU wanna do it, for yourself and NO ONE ELSE!

DR DAVID STARKEY

My mother always used to say, "David, you may be of a superior intelligence to everyone else on this beleaguered planet of ours, but that tongue of yours will surely be the ruin of you!" Little did that poor misguided female know that the aforesaid appendage would in fact be the making of me! As the world now acknowledges, the Starkey Tongue — marvellously pink and moist, enviably mobile, with a devilishly powerful sting when aroused — has made me one of the most talked-about figures in the Western World. Only yesterday, the *Daily Express* granted me substantial space really very high up on page 5 to consider the rights and wrongs, from a neo-Voltairian perspective, of the new-look Berlei booster brassiere. And just two days before that, the famous Starkey Tongue had made a well-received guest appearance on Radio

Clyde to deliver the perspective of a distinguished social historian on the new Schwarznegger "movie".

And here's a little exclusive for you: plans for the immortalisation of the Starkey Tongue are already well afoot. A fervent admirer — let us, for the sake of argument, call him "Dr D.S." — has written to the Director General of the BBC (a Mr John Birt) officially to echo the widespread view that the Corporation should honour its most valued practitioner in the fashion most appropriate. "A sculpture of the Starkey Tongue in pliable rubber, three metres by twelve metres, moistened 24 hours a day by electronic water-ducts, is long overdue. The foyer of Broadcasting House is positively crying out for it. It would be the envy of the world. Will you not now show the moral courage to comply with a nation's needs, you wretched imbecile?"

❖

"You wretched imbecile!" It is for this type of deliciously caustic remark that the Starkey Tongue has gained its international renown. My waspish put-downs have become legendary, to be quoted wheresoever in the world high intelligence is afforded its true respect. Savour, for instance:

To a little old lady collecting money for the poor: "Shove off, you ghastly collection of ill-assorted and increasingly decrepid molecules — and take your inelegant collecting box with you! It makes me want to vomit!"

To a 'leading heart' surgeon: "I put it to you that you would rather beat an innocent baby to a pulp than get your stubby little fingers dirty by saving a life — answer me that one, go on, answer it, you dolt, you can't can you, I said you can't can you? Pah! It makes me want to vomit! Game, set and match to Starkey!"

To a 'tireless' aid worker: "Doesn't he genuinely make you want to vomit — his dogoodery, his awful *niceness*, his endless look-at-me-I'm-so-bloody-tirelessness? It makes me want to vomit!"

A gem every time! Can one think of a single other accredited academic who has made such a distinguished name for himself as The Rudest Man in Britain on mid-morning talk radio? Of course one can't! To my certain knowledge, Sir Geoffrey Elton hasn't even appeared on the Household Tip slot of The Big Breakfast, let alone featured on the double-page Celebrity Bathroom spread in *YOU* magazine! Yet he possesses the infernal impudence to call himself an historian! Frankly, it makes me want to vomit!

❖

Of my many academic hats, the one I find most profitable to wear is that of the Leading Constitutional Expert. If, say, a major national newspaper wants a Leading Constitutional Expert to test-drive the new Alfa Romeo or comment on the latest gravity-defying garment worn by — ooh, don't! — Miss Pamela Anderson, then it is to Dr David Starkey that they instantly turn.

As you well know, I am a regular fixture on BBC2's widely-respected Newsnight programme. Incidentally, I rib Jeremy (Paxman) mercilessly both on and off the air! Only last month, he asked me to comment on the future of the Royal Family under a divorced monarch from a constitutional perspective. "How dare you prance into this studio and ask me impertinent questions about the Constitution, you tall, dark interrogator, you!" I responded, quick as a flash. I then paused for effect before adding, "You make me want to vomit!" Result? Two inches of coverage (plus mugshot) on page six of the next day's *Daily Mirror* — not to mention a suitably irate reader's letter in the *Daily Mail*! How wrong you proved to be, Mother — how very wrong you proved to be!

❖

Envious detractors, and, sad to say, there are many such mischievous reptiles, accuse me of intellectual name-dropping, and of presenting cliché in the guise of bogus paradox. To them I say further from the truth nothing could be, for nothing could be further from the truth. To be frank, I have long detested those who ride on the coat-tails of greater minds; I am with Wittgenstein, Montaigne and La Rochefoucauld on this.

They also accuse me of sadism and cruelty. This is really very naughty of them, very naughty indeed — smacky botties all round, methinks! Any halfway competent geneticist will confirm that it is not my fault that I combine a very strong analytical intelligence with an exceedingly powerful verbal intelligence. But cruel? Never! Witness my warmth and kindness in dealing with my colleague Janet Daley when she popped into the Moral Maze studio to be on The David Starkey show this week. Janet tends to "go on a bit", as Shakespeare might have put it — and it takes all my powers of tact and diplomacy to save her from herself.

Janet Daley: We all have a moral responsibility for our —
Dr David Starkey: — a typically fatuous comment, if I may say so, Janet!
Janet Daley: If you'll just let me fin —
Dr David Starkey: — nish. May I now broaden out the discussion a little, Michael? Why is Janet wearing that perfectly ghastly mimsy-pimsy floral dress?

And thus with one fell swoop I silenced the poor benighted female for a precious few minutes — saving her the embarrassment that would undoubtedly have accrued from her silly little observations! Cruel? No, I would never call myself that. Unless, of course, the editor of *The Sun* is offering proper reimbursement for it.

Away with you all, now. I think I want to vomit. Is there a studio available?

GEORGE STEINER

Concomitantly, silence is, as I have pointed out in pioneering work in many books and seminars, invariably quarried and pillaged by lesser minds (usually without acknowledgement and certainly without apology), golden.

Cities, towns, conurbations, large groups of buildings placed near or proximate to one another to form a definable whole, are both the conduits and the receptacles for noise, sound, *clamour* (*klamari* in Swahili, *calamari* in Italian, though I prefer the *cannelloni*). At regular time period intervals, I retreat to the French hillsides with my distinguished yet unspoken wife, to breathe in the silence, unloud and noiseless, that was once partaken by the by no means lesser minds of Flaubert and Racine.

Maritally, we sit in a fieldly meadow in an incipiently quiet time/space continuum observing the hush (*huss* in Somali) stretching far beneath us, down to the herd, team, group of cows below. "Ah, silence!" I exclaim exclamatorily in simple wonderment, "Silence — the silence that is with us now — a silence golden as James's *Bowl*, as Apuleius's *Asse*, as Frazer's *Bough*, that silence blessed by my original study, now translated into fifteen languages, taken up yet still not acknowledged by those whose academic reputations fall sadly short of my own. Ah, silence! A void, a circumstantial gap, a vivid diaspora, the sound, rare and provocative, created when one's talk ceases. Silence, both metaphysical and actual, both concomitant and —"

"Moo!" enunciates a cow, bovine and cowlike, and the other cows follow suitly, "Moo! Moo! Moo!".

My antennae, exceedingly alert, like a *lieder* by Schubert or a poem by Pound, inform me that this cuddish interruption is part of a Friesian conspiracy intent on placing in jeopardy my seminar on the nature of *la silencia*. These animals possess all the professional jealousy and unctuous mooishness of the Oxford-educated. They have been put up to their loutish intervention by those in the English faculty less honoured than myself.

"Shoo! Shoo! Shoo!" I interpolate.

"Moo! Moo! Moo!" they respond.

I seize the opportunity to point out to my unspoken wife that in the Oubangi language there are fifteen words meaning "moo", only one of them in common use by cows. But she cannot hear me. She has her ear-plugs in (*arapluggi* in Cameroon), as she has done since 1974, still perversely intent upon listening to the mute, smothering silence that lies somewhere beyond words.

❖

Regrets? Maria Callas once sang that she regretted the Rhine, that inexhaustibly damp yet geographically constrained river. Though others may find it hard, difficult, *difficile* to imagine, I have been burdened lumberingly with personal regrets, to each of which I pride myself on being sufficiently humble to confess. My failings are plenitude. I regret, for instance, having yet to re-read Dante's *Inferno* in Icelandic. I regret that none of my pupils, for all their undoubted industry in the appropriation of my ideas (always covertly, never gratefully) have nevertheless found themselves unable to match the breadth, the depth, the width or the temperature of my learning, and their minds remain unequipped with diving boards or changing rooms. I regret failing to learn Mokoan to a standard sufficiently high to translate some of my own Mokoan verse, now incidentally highly collectable (I recently saw no less than 20 unopened copies in the burgeoning Steiner section of a prestigious secondhand bookdealers), into Tibetan and from Tibetan back into the original Finnish. And I regret my failure to stand, owing to pressure of thinking, for the Presidencies of France, Germany or America — or all simultaneously, had their citizens demanded it. And I sometimes regret that my pre-eminence in so many fields has led to me to neglect others, which have consequently suffered a drop in their prestige.

❖

What is a wall with no writing upon it? I would not know, as I have yet to see one. Yet there is little of any purposeful use and/or useful purpose in the world in the last decade of the second millennium. The sloppy armies of Barbaria are on their ill-shodden march, dragging civilisation headlongly to its doom. In the United States of America, the President's daughter is pictured dancing at a "night-club discotheque". In South-East Asia, the Spice Girls appear on daytime television, yet Gustav Mahler continues to be denied his own show. In Switzerland, Heinz Baked Beans make inroads into the supermarket shelves. In England, few schoolchildren are fluent in twelve languages before the age of nine. Instead, they watch television programmes like "Oasis" and gyrate to the primitive sexual rhythms, at once tribal and solipsistic, of The Teletubbies, none of whom, save perhaps La-La, could hold down a post at any major European University.

❖

Alas, our civilisation is on the run from the emancipatory strains of the intellect. For why else but for fear would such a first-grade thinker as myself, a thinker who has thunk more thoughts than all the rest of them put together, be at once so vilified, so ignored, so up-covered?

AN AUDIENCE WITH
ROD STEWART

(Rod enters. Applause. More applause. Rod turns round and wiggles his bottom at the audience. Standing ovation)

Rod: Woooh! *(Pause)* Nah, bollocks!

Audience: Hahahahahahahaha!

Rod: Wooh! Any ques-tee-o-nez, nah? Make it all above board, will ya?! Nah. Bollocks!

Audience: Hahahahahahahahahaha!

Rod: Me old mate, the late, great Ronnie Wood! The legendary Woody! Rock 'n' roll! Nah! Yeah, mate?

Woody: Burp! Gorra bidda wind, Rod! Hahahahaha!

Audience: Hahahahahahahahaha.

(Wolf whistles)

Woody: Burp! Nah, Rod, wodda wonnid to arse wuz — air ye doin, mate?

Rod: Couldn't arf do wiv a right good shaggin', mate! Nah! Bollocks!

(Raucous laughter. Standing ovation)

Rod: Here's a song written by me old mate wossisname — the crafty old shagger!!! Nah!

Ah m say-lin
Ah m say-lin
Harm gen crass d seey
Ah m say-lin
Starmy wart tuz
T b wiv yer
T be freey
Ah m flar-yin
Ah m flar-yin
Harm gen crass d seey

(Applause. More applause. Cheers. Catcalls)

Rod: Wooh! Yeah! Anyone gorra quessie for me? Yeah — the bird in the third row with the nice tits! Ha! Ha! You smooth-talkin' ladykiller, Rod, you! Nah!

(Laughter. Applause)

Ulrika Jonsson: Rod...

Rod: Hi, darlin'!

Audience: Hahahahahahahaha!

Ulrika Jonsson: Rod, what's the most fun you've ever had ever in the whole of your life in the entire history of the world bar none?

Rod: Can't beat a good shaggin', love! Nah, seerzly, lez think, I dunno, I carn answer that, nah —

Woody: You old goat, Rod, mate!!

(Laughter. Applause)

Rod: Down boy! Hahahaha! Nah! Great mate — lays an gennelmen — the legendary Woody!

(Applause)

Rod: Please wowcum — Baby Spice!

(Applause)

Rod *(singing)*: Cumarn angel ma harse on far

Baby Spice *(singing)*: En doan denar yermar desaar

Rod: Spread y wins and lemme carm insaard

Both: Tonaarght's the naarght!
   Tonaarght's the naarght!
   Sgonnabe yallraaaaght!
   Tonaarght's the naarght!
   Tonaarght's the naarght!

Rod: Wooh!

(Standing ovation. Catcalls)

(Sings)
   Way kup Mageh ar thing
   Ar gos umfin ter say chew
   Slay Setember an ah
   Really shoobe backa skoo

(Applause. Yells. Catcalls)

Desmond Lynam: Rod, despite all your success, you've managed to remain an ordinary bloke with both feet firmly on the ground. How d'you manage it?

Rod: I shag the wife somethin' rotten! Hahahaha! Wicked! Nah, seerzly, I'm a normal bloke, like my birds, like a glass or six of the old boozey-woozey...

Woody: Make mine a pint, Rod! Hahahaha!

(Audience cheers and laughter)

Rod: The legendary Mister Ronnie Wood, lays an gennelmen! Nah, but we live a normal life, go darn the pub. Well, we don't actually go darn the pub, nah, we get the landlord to dismantle the pub, bring it to our place in a container lorry and reassemble it at our place, just for the sake of convenience, know what I mean? Nah. Here's one yer might recognise. Cheers.

Rod *(sings):* Dooyer thin Karm sek see
Just ree chout an tarch me
Carmon baby lair me know

(Wiggles bottom. Applause, more applause)

Rod: Bollocks! Hahahahahaha! Ta-ra! See you darn the boozer! Hahahahaha! Classic!

(Audience rise to their feet, cheering and clapping. Camera pans round celebrity audience of Rod's contemporaries, all swaying in rough time to the beat, including Alan Freeman, Jimmy Savile, Angela Rippon, Douglas Hurd, Janet Street-Porter, Quintin Hailsham, Kenneth Kendall and Penelope Keith)

JANET STREET PORTER'S MEN:
WILL SELF & DAVE STEWART

Janet Street-Porter: Totally mega-brill you two amazing
  guys could schlepp in here today, 'cos you're two of the
  most fan-bloody-tastic mega-success stories in youth
  culture today. Totally amazing, Dave, you must be over
  the bloody moon with your success. I mean, it must make
  you wanna boogie all night long, like totally get down
  and get with it, you know what I mean, guys?

Dave Stewart: It's like a total nightmare. I mean like even
  when I was a kid I like felt sort of TRAPPED, you know.
  Like, perhaps I was wearing a blue pullover but what I
  really wanted to wear was a green pullover, so I like felt
  sort of TRAPPED in the blue pullover, and that.

Will Self: Like Wittgenstein, I feel very serendipitous to the
  conceptual synaesthesia of Dave's semiological dilemma,
  as Camus once said, but then in many ways I have

sympathy with existentialism, as is clear from a close textual analysis of that extraordinary passage in my last book, "Chop It Off", where the 90-year-old tramp has nothing to stir his tea with so he cuts off his own penis, then, finding he has no penis, cuts off his big toe and grafts it on in its place with a slice of Dairylea.

Dave Stewart: Heavy number.

❖

Janet Street-Porter: You guys are so bloody brill, you really are. What's it like to be a genius, Dave?

Dave Stewart: Nightmare, basically. Like, every morning, I wake up and think, "What a nightmare. I just woke up". Then I go back to sleep. And then I'm really fucked 'cos I'm not awake.

Janet Street-Porter: That's a pretty uncool trip, Dave, like a —

Dave Stewart: Nightmare.

Janet Street-Porter: That's it. Nightmare.

Dave Stewart: Then when I'm asleep, I might have a nightmare, and that's a, like —

Janet Street-Porter: Nightmare?

Dave Stewart: Nightmare, yeah.

Will Self: Heidigger.

Janet Street-Porter: Heidi?

Will Self: Heidigger.

Janet Street-Porter: Oh, hi!

❖

Janet Street Porter: The thing that's totally mega-brill about you guys is the way you, you know, like do the zeitgeist.

Will Self: Mallarmé.

Janet Street Porter: Know it well. "Wake up, Maggie, I think I got somethin' to say to you!". Love it. Very seventies. I'm deeply into the whole nostalgia thing. It's so modern.

Dave Stewart: Can be a nightmare if you look at it in a different way. I mean, like, I've had twenty top ten singles and I'm like a big success and I got all this money

but whenever I like want to get from one end of the
room to another I still have to walk, or crawl. Walk or
crawl. Whichever. There's no way out. And sometimes
I'm sitting down, and then I stand and I think, god, I'm
putting all this creative energy just into not falling over,
into balancing on these two feet, and it's such a waste,
it's, like, a total —

Janet Street Porter: Nightmare.

Dave Stewart: Right.

❖

Janet Street Porter: The thing that really things me about
you two guys is that you really, you know, thingy the
feelings of a generation.

Will Self: "Articulate?"

Janet Street Porter: That too.

Will Self: I think we're living in a continuum.

Janet Street Porter: We're all part of the continuum of
Europe, what with joining the Common Market and that.
How do you feel, Will, about the artist's role in this new
sort of quotes "Thingy sort of" close quotes society?

Will Self: Frankly, it fucks me up and screws my head to
the floor and then pisses on it from a great height. The
British have never liked their novelists to be hierophantic
decocters of augural spectograms, in the postlapserian
sense, and it frightens British society as a whole when one
of us has the quasi-Dostolevskian nerve to acknowledge
that he is at a cultural and semiological apex of a
semiological post-Freudian structural seismic shift in
perceptions, in the same way it would frighten them, vis à
vis being frightened, if I were to rip off my left ear and
eat it with a splurge of ketchup before spewing it up all
over the walls and then writing my name in it with my
outstretched tongue. So what they are driven to do is to
crush the artist's testicles until the pus runs out. And then
lick it all up.

Janet Street Porter: Amazing image. Totally memorable. The guy's a genius. And like, as another total bloody mega genius, Dave, what's your idea of fun?

Dave Stewart: When I was a child, six or seven, I sometimes got an ice-lolly from a so-called grown-up. And I'd really look forward to this ice-lolly, like for weeks, but then when I'd got it I'd find that if you left it out in the sun for a long time, like an hour or more, it'd melt, so eventually it wouldn't be there any more. And I thought that was a real downer, it really freaked me out. Now every time I see an ice-lolly I totally identify with that ice-lolly, I'm like melting and I have to go and sit in the freezer compartment of my fridge with like a stick up my arse. But that's not fun. It's more of a er —

Janet Street Porter: Nightmare. Right.

❖

Janet Street Porter: What fascinates me about both of you is that you're totally ideas driven, you guys know what makes people tick.

Dave Stewart: They're not all tick. Some are, like, pretty clever really, which is just as worrying in a different way.

Will Self: I can't eat a packet of crisps without thinking of its metaphoric, semaphoric and sophomorphic implications. It's as if every crisp is a slice of deep-fried sick, and that's how post-Watergate society drags itself about like a decapitated nun, vis à vis death and disfigurement. I switch in on Wittgenstein's vision of a post-holocaust buggy-ride there.

Dave Stewart: Real downer.

Janet Street Porter: I bet you two guys are great in bed too! Lorluvaduck! Talk about giving great infotainment! You're really hot and mega and you're so modern you make me wanna boogie! Ciao!

SIR ROY STRONG

MARCH 18TH 1974: The Queen Mother is no beauty, bless her. She is even, dare I say it, a bit *common*, with a perfectly ghastly habit of interrupting one when one is talking of subjects beyond her. Bidden to luncheon at Clarence House — a reasonably serviceable London *pied-à-terre*, if fearfully ugly — I suspect I rather frightened her with my compelling mixture of historical erudition, intellectual breadth, conversational agility and sheer *razzle-dazzle*. But she was obviously so thrilled to talk to me that one can forgive her much, if not everything.

Thank heavens for my rare *panache*. I held the table — a dull philosopher and his dreary wife; a ghastly, spineless politician (possibly the Prime Minister?) and his equally ghastly wife; a couple of vulgarly famous film stars and a boorish poet — utterly spellbound with all the latest gossip from the Victoria and Albert Museum. Apparently, the Keeper of Ceramics has fallen out with the Under-Keeper of Miniatures after hearing that one of the Secretaries in Stuffed Animals had mentioned that the Director of Engravings had taken a dislike to an early work by the Assistant Director of Porcelain.

Inevitably, this news rendered the table speechless. It was the Queen Mother who was the first to chip in. Alas, she was desperately muddled.

"And apparently they all absolutely *loathe* the new Director," she said. "They say he's a self-serving, publicity-mad, social-climbing ponce."

"Correction, ma'am!" I laughed. "You must be thinking of someone else. You see, *I* am the new Director!"

Poor dear, she gets her names very mixed up these days. The food, incidentally, was filthy. Needless to say, I received many admiring glances for my broad-brimmed scarlet fedora and purple crushed velvet knickerbockers, not unmixed with a certain amount of envy from the ladies.

JUNE 7TH 1980: HRH The Princess of Wales, Princess Alexandra, HM The Queen, Lord Charteris, Lady Antonia Fraser, Lady Hartwell, President Giscard d'Estaing, Jackie Onassis, Sir Isaiah Berlin, The Duke and Duchess of Buccleuch, Lord Rothschild: how they all admire one, and how well they look in one's index.

JULY 12TH 1983: The new Pope has no taste in clothes. Whatever virtues he has, dress sense is not one of them. Doesn't the poor poppet realise that crucifixes are *passé* and that (*don't!*) stiff white collars are dreadfully *sixties*?

I have served close-on a decade now at the V&A. It is widely recognised that I have achieved more than any other human being of my own or other generations in any field, at any time. My "Voici La Roy" exhibition was an outstanding success, and Princess Margaret was not alone in deeming my lavish "Cravats from the Strong Collection" one of the most memorable exhibitions of cravats she had ever set eyes on.

But time marches on, and I feel I must seek pastures new. Many close friends have suggested that the Papacy is quite simply *crying out* for a candidate of my calibre to knock it into some sort of style. Norman (St John Stevas) says he will have a word with Grey (Gowrie) to persuade Peter (Carrington) to put my name forward to his good friends in the Vatican.

Of course, the whole thing needs a thorough overhaul. As Pope, my first action would be to improve the food. Even a few dabs of *salsa verde* would perk up those wafers no end, and the house wine is at present *execrable*. And then I would set about the clothes. I have been thinking of Regency velvet jackets, ruffled shirts and dreamy flared crushed-velvet loon-pants for my Cardinals, and black damask skirted jackets with high side-vents and turtle-necks for my Bishops. I wonder whether one could persuade HRH Princess Margaret to act as one's Papal Nuncio to Belgravia and surrounding parishes? I must have a word with Princess Michael, to see what she thinks.

MAY 17TH 1989: To a finger-supper with the blessed Sir Harold Acton at *La Pietra*. Tony Snowdon in a lime-green *blouson* with high-standing sleeves, tightly waisted matelot jacket and sky-blue brushed silk *pantalons*. Dicky Buckle collars me and says that Binkie Beaumont really hates Cecil Beaton. Later, Binkie Beaumont shepherds me into a corner to tell me that Cecil Beaton really hates Dicky Buckle. As brandy is served (certainly *not* five star) Cecil asks if he can have a word. Apparently, Dicky Buckle really hates Binkie

Beaumont. And they all really hate Harold.

A divine evening of friendship and warmth in the company of angels. Ascending les escaliers to my room, I realise that I forgot to tell them that the Assistant Keeper of Manuscripts has fallen out — and most severely — with the Curator of the Chinese Collection. Ah well — it will be something to surprise them with tomorrow.

MARCH 5TH 1995: A fearfully busy time in the gardener's yearbook. Our own *jardin* is home to twenty-two varieties of different leek, all planted in such a way as to echo the distinctive shape of my moustaches. I am a great one for monuments. People say that I am a monomaniac, but these are strictly divided between my own achievements (three and a half acres) and those of the rest of the world (quarter of an acre). One also has special tombs to one's darling dear departed pussies — The Reverend Wenceslas Muff, His Grace the Rt Rev Raving Woofter, Archdeacon Silly Wanker and Prebendary Raddled Old Twat — alongside commemorative beds to my very dear friends HRH Princess Margaret (33 varieties of stinging nettle) and Sir John Pope-Hennessy (compost heap). In the far corner, there's an abundant hedge, skilfully cropped to form an exact replica of Michelangelo's David, though with the addition of a beautiful, droopy moustache, ravishing shoulder-length hair and distinctive circular spectacles.

Recently, I have extended my *jardin* away from the limits of the grounds to a commemorative plantation on my face. The crop of sweet peas in the area between my lips and my much-admired nose is coming along famously, though it's still early days for the brussels sprouts seeding in my silvery locks. Not long now, and I shall have to open myself to the general public. "Circumspice" is my motto. Or should that be "Circumspivvy"?

QUENTIN TARANTINO

I ain't talkin' my ass outta this shit, no way man. You wanna diary, like you git a diary, no hassle, aright? You seen my latest movie, you seen it? How many times you seen it? It's even better on the seventeenth, aright, no shit.

Like, wodever, the new movie's todally fuckin' different from my other movies, aright, like it's more fuckin' tender and lovin' for one. There's this great tender scene, aright, when this guy like holds a pistol up the nostril of this girl right and he ever so delicately blasts it fuckin' off, great scene, man, nostril all over the fuckin' wall, but — and here's the tender bit, aright — he doesn't blast off the other nostril, he lets her keep it, aright, 'cos he's like completing the learning curve of like coming to terms with himself like and his position in society and his responsibilities as a fellow human being aright? Sal-fuckin-vation, man, no shit.

❖

Like tough titties, man. I ain't gonna take no fuckin' insults, not from you not from any fuckin' body, no way, aright? So when a smartass reviewer from the New York Fuckin' Times says like this latest movie is my best movie yet I turn round and say look you fuckin' fuckass how can you expect me to deal with a fucking statement like that, man, you know what I'm saying, who's gonna put up with that shit, like, is he saying my other two movies weren't so good, is that what he's fuckin' sayin', well, is he? 'Cos if that's what he's fuckin' sayin', I got a problem with that, like, uhuh, so's maybe it is my best fuckin' movie yet, but the other two movies were my best fuckin' movies yet too, no shit. So you take that fuckin' insult back, you cocksuckin' smartass critic, or I'll baadass your brains, motherfucker.

❖

Don't talk to me about morality, man. I got more morality up my fuckin' ass than like you got in your head, man. Moral centre? I got an extremely moral centre, like in Reservoir Dogs — how many times you seen Reservoir Dogs — great ain't it? — like in Reservoir Dogs when the guy with the cattle prod up his ass whips the other guy till the blood spurts out all over the third guy's nice clean shirt and this makes the third guy like so shitass angry, aright, he slices off the first guy's toes with this like samurai sword right, so like now if that's not moral aright, you don't know nothing 'bout morality 'cos like the fourth guy, he's somewhere else, he don't do nothing bad, so nothin' bad happens to him, aright, until a whole lot later in the movie when he winds up gettin' castrated by like a food processor or wodever, like it's a kinda Christian, kinda Old

154

Testamenty kinda thingish kinda thing, aright, but *deep*.

❖

I'm not saying I'm better than like Welles and John Ford
and David Lean and Kubrick and all that kinda shit, no way
man, but like you wanna know what, they didn't know
much about movies, that's all I'm saying, no shit, aright?
Like that scene in Brief Encounter, where the tweedy
cocksucker and the woman are in the Burger King on the
station platform or wodever? Well, Lean missed it, man, he
totally missed it like NOTHIN' HAPPENS, no
redemption, no guns, no nothing. So now I'm usin' the
same scene in my next movie, aright, only this time it's like
for real and I've retitled the movie Brief Total Fuckup:

OLD WOMAN: Oh Charles! Oh... Charles!

OLD MAN: Oh, Jean! Oh... Jean!

*(Cedric bursts into restaurant. Cedric takes out his gun and
shoots Old Man three times in the chest, blowing him out of his
chair)*

OLD WOMAN: Oh, Charles! Oh... Charles!

*(Old Woman has shit her pants. Cedric empties his gun on
her. Blood shoots out her ears. Cedric picks up her cheese and
tomato sandwich. Wipes blood off it with his sleeve, finishes it
in two bites)*

OLD MAN *(reviving)*: Hggnnn! Hnnnggg!

CEDRIC: Shut your fuckin' mouth, motherfucker!

*(Cedric whistles "Remember You're a Womble", pulls out
pickaxe and bludgeons Old Man to death. Train pulls into
station. Cedric boards it and leaves the station a free man)*

See what I'm sayin'? Cedric has been redeemed, aright,
'cos he like remembered to wipe the blood off the sandwich
before eating it, uhuh, just like his momma always teached

him. See, my films are about redemption, and, like I said,
I'm a totally and very morally centred human being, aright?

❖

The thing about my movies is like they're just fuckin'
great movies, aright, like I don't buy into this whole fuckin'
idea that if you show a movie that's like violent you're
gonna like get a whole lotta people in a violent-type
situation with people's noses being shot off and their hands
all crushed like on the ground and holes through their chests
aright just because they've been like watching Fred
Flintstone or wodever, like real messy. Like my movies,
sure they're violent, I like violence in movies, fact I wish
there was more, 'cos violence is real not like that Jane
Austen Merchant Ivory shit, like Pardon Me, Mr Bennett,
says Young Emma, take this you badaass motherfucker, Mr
Bennett you and Mrs Bennett ain't talkin' your ass out of
this shit, you know what I'm sayin', no way. Hell, I
watched 10,000, maybe 100,000 movies since I was a fuckin'
teenager but they never made me violent, aright, no way, I
said they never made me fuckin' violent or abusive or any of
these thingy fuckin' things, did you say something?! So
don't say they fuckin' did, man, or I'll blow your fuckin'
head off, two, three shots, easy, aright? Get the fuck outta
here if you're gonna be like that man — that's no fuckin'
way to treat a fuckin' genius type film-maker artist, uh-uh!

NORMAN TEBBIT

C herie. That's not a Christian name I often hear as I walk the bulldog down my tree-lined avenue. Far from it. You hear plenty of good, trusty British names. Bert. Dave. Fred. John. Jane. Judy. Eileen. Yes, and even Norman. But — forgive me — I can't once recall a Cherie.

"Hurry up, Cherie!", "Hands out of pockets, Cherie!", "You'll get a sound spanking, Cherie, when your Dad gets home!". "Take your coloured friend elsewhere — I'll not have him in this house, Cherie!"

Doesn't sound quite right, does it?

Could this be because Cherie is not a 100% British name after all? Sounds foreign to me. Cherry, yes. Cherie, no.

To my ordinary British ear, the word has a peculiar,

almost Eastern, ring to it. Frankly, it wouldn't surprise me to find it had pitched up from India or even Pakistan. I am no expert, but to me the word Cherie suggests all-night Biryanis, beggars on street-corners, cholera, foul-smelling joss-sticks and skinny old men in National Health Specs wearing next-to-nothing telling us how to live our lives before being filmed 40 years later by overweight bleeding-heart touchy-feely wishy-washy liberal cry-babies like the self-styled Lord "Dickie" Attenborough.

Of course, if the trendy new Prime Minister of this once-great country chooses to run around with an Indian wife, that is his own concern.

But doesn't it get on your goat — as it does on mine — that the so-called People's Prime Minister can't come clean about his predilections? A word in your ear, Blair. Isn't it high time you forced your Missus into a sari? Oh, and don't forget to lock up those valuables when she finds her way indoors!

❖

I bow to no man in my admiration of our true British Spice Girls. They are set to conquer the world, and good luck to them. In my book, they are an excellent advertisement for Great Britain.

Ginger Spice: full of bounce. Posh Spice: very stylish. Baby Spice: what a very pleasant young lady. Sporty Spice: very trim and fit.

All well and good. But to my mind there's one Spice Girl who sticks out like a sore thumb. You know who I'm talking about.

Scary Spice.

Who the hell let her in? Would someone please be kind enough to tell me the point of this woman — if woman she be?

Her hair is neither straight nor wavy. I would call it

crinkly myself. Her lips show tell-tale signs of plumpness. And — put it this way — if I were her, I'd sue the manufacturer of my sun-bed for his failure to include an "off" switch with that particular model.

Don't get me wrong. I harbour no grudge against our Friends from Overseas.

But there must be a limit. All this alien behaviour — and now we learn she has a ring through her tongue!

An honest British fiver — none of this ecu nonsense, por favor! — for the first man to tie a rope in it and lead Scary Spice back to whatever godforsaken land she hails from!

❖

Those meddlesome Eurocrats really do have it in for the good old British motorway pile-up.

Now they have the brass nerve to tell us to drive slower in order to cut down on our cherished pile-ups — particularly in foggy weather.

Sorry, Miguel. Driving slower has never been the British way. Never has been — never will be.

It comes as no surprise that the Heseltines and Clarkes of this world have rushed to embrace this latest example of Euro-lunacy like sodomites on shore leave rushing to embrace black sailors in dark alleyways. Snug for some. But not for me.

Small wonder they turn their toffee-noses up at honest-to-goodness British fog. When the weather gets tough, these Euro-smoothies are more used to jetting off to foreign climes in their chauffeur-driven limousines. Not like the rest of us, who are forced to turn an honest penny at home.

Nothing wrong with a bit of British fog. Nothing wrong with driving like a real man in all weathers.

And if it results in a pile-up, so much the better. It's one British tradition I'm not prepared to surrender to the Euroninnies. *On yer bike, Jose — and smack into the oncoming traffic, s'il vous plaît.*

❖

I see a film about Oscar Wilde is playing at my local Odeon. Would it not be more worthwhile to honour a true British hero, such as Sir Douglas Bader or Margaret Thatcher?

It's yet another example, I fear, of the limp-wristed brigade hosing us from the rooftops with their unsavoury message.

Sodomy. Not a nice word, is it? Sounds foreign to me.

And its meaning's not all that nice, either.

Let me put it in words of one syllable. It means two blokes removing their suits and ties and touching one another all over, even getting into bed together and going the whole hog — tongues, knees, fingers and heaven knows what else — before wriggling and rolling and yelping with pleasure, and begging and panting for more at the top of their voices.

That's not my cup of tea. Never has been, never will be.

Incidentally, I see that the trendy powers-that-be are letting another of these unsavoury types into the country to spread his noxious message at the Royal Albert Hall. Nana Mouskouri is the name. I need hardly remind you that this is the well-known Greek gentleman who prefers to wear his hair long and prance around in ladies' frocks.

No doubt, Mr Blair and his nancy-boy acolytes approve of such Euro-antics. Personally, I will be giving the Festival Hall a wide berth on the night in question. No doubt Mr Mouskouri will occupy himself that evening by casting his bespectacled eyes over some poor fellow's buttocks.

But I can promise you this. They sure as hell won't be mine.

THANK YOU FOR THE MUSIC: FAVOURITE ABBA SONGS

GWYNETH PALTROW: Agnetha, Benny, Bjorn, Anni-Frid — I want you to — I want you to know — oh, I so want you to know how much — I'm sorry — I want you to know how much I've always loved — truly loved — your wonderful, wonderful music — more than you'll ever — oh — ever know. My favourite is my dear grandpa's favourite and my mom's favourite and my dead cousin Keith's favourite and I feel it would have been the favourite of — of Abraham Lincoln had he — had he been able to be with us today and please God let's not forget Martin Luther King who was a truly great man, truly he was — and so our all-time favourite Abba song is — and it was such a — such a very difficult choice — and I thank my dead great-uncle Henry and my dead great-aunt Hattie and everyone who's ever lived or died for giving me the — the — courage to make the decision on all our behalfs — but it just has to be *Gimme Gimme Gimme (A Man After Midnight)*. And Nelson Mandela — this one — this one's for — I'm sorry, I'm just overcome — this one's for YOU. And thank you, America, for giving us Abba. You're beautiful.

ROY JENKINS: I suppose, on reflection, it is safe to say that future historians will lay the vast international success of the popular music combination "Abba" firmly at my door. The vair real popularity of toe-tapping tunes such as *Ring Ring, Money Money Money* and *Mama Mia* would surely have been impossible had it not been for my not, I think, wholly unsuccessful period as Home Secretary. Nevertheless — and bearing in mind something L.B.J. said to me during a private meeting in his personal sitting room at The White House — I would stick my neck out and nominate *Voulez-Vous* as my vair favourite Abba tune of all time. Though I never found the time to meet Benny and Bjorn on a personal basis, a close reading of *Voulez-Vous* will suggest to future historians that the two of them had spent some vair considerable time perusing my "Essays and Speeches" (1981) in which, in all modesty, I offer my long-awaited advice to the French peoples on future social and monetary reforms.

JEANETTE WINTERSON: I close my beautiful brown eyes, shut tight as only tightly-shut shutty-tighters can ever be, and my imagination — mangled nation, natty man, animated asian — plays me *Dancing Queen* over and over and over again on a personal stereo steered solely by love and art. No one sings it, wings it, tings it, like me, alone and rejected, howling Abba in the tyrannous wilderness of my room. My lips meet those of Agnetha. Scarlet. Moist. Swedish. We sigh for the world. For the world we sigh.

JEFFREY ARCHER: I was privileged to have been a member of Abba from 1974-1979, and under the pseudonym of Bjeffrey I was the lead singer on their major worldwide hits *Fernando* and *Dancing Queen*, which remain my all-time favourites to this day. Incidentally, it may interest you to know that I was at that time the only member of Abba to also have gained two Olympic gold medals for my country in lacrosse and free-form skating.

GORE VIDAL: As the deprived and disappointingly small-membered citizens of a sub-literate Third World country, few Britons can begin to grasp the true meaning behind the most memorable of all Abba phonographs, *I Do I Do I Do I Do*. It takes no great understanding of Our Masters to realise that this is in fact a subliminal message from the international firearms industry. By echoing the sound of a high velocity machine-gun — *I-Do-I-Do-I-Do-I-Do* — the firearms lobby seeks to influence the people of the United States of America and Ungreat Britain(!) into siding with them against President Bill Clinton, who they wish to besmirch for refusing to murder small children under the name of patriotism. And the name of the Judge in the O.J. Simpson trial? *Ito*. Even the haphazardly-coiffed and semi-numerate Einstein could have put two and two together on that one. Incidentally, though no great admirer of pink silk against Swedish buttock, I would nominate Benny as my all-time favourite Abba member. His smile has the faintest whiff of my hallowed friend President John F. Kennedy, who once attempted to kiss me in the Oval Office — with no little success, might I add.

JOHN PRESCOTT: Let's make no bones about it, *All What It Is The Winner Takes* must be surely the ever greatest Abba track of time all, not to mention *The Game of the Name*, which is even better let's not argue with facts because they're there to be questioned, they were a group great all the same.

MOHAMED AL FAYED: I have the greatest pleasure in submitting to your gracious request for my top three Abba songs of all time. Please find my top three as stated below:

1) *Chiquifuggintita*
2) *Knowing Me Fuggin You*
3) *Mama Fuggin Mia*
4) *Fernanfuggindo*
5) *Super Fuggin Trouper*

GERMAINE GREER: For Chrissake, what's so great about Benny and Bjorn? Angry? Too bloody right I am. It's high time we acknowledged the truly extraordinary contribution of Agnetha and Anna-Frid. I first heard *Waterloo* in 1974. It's become the anthem of all those women who prefer not to spend six hours a day scrubbing their husbands' toilets. And while the women in Abba were singing their bloody GUTS out, the men were just sitting there like mindless apes, counting out their cash. And surveys have shown that after they'd finished singing, Agnetha and Anna-Frid were forced to do all the bloody clearing up — piling the drums into the vans, polishing the guitars, etcetera — while the men just lay around in their satin bloody jumpsuits picking at their beards. But for Chrissake, what's so great about Agnetha and Anna-Frid? If the Women's Movement still means anything, it means it's high time we acknowledged the tremendous suffering caused to women by those two painted caterwauling so-called singers. Angry? Too bloody right I am.

LADY THATCHER'S
HONG KONG DIARY

To dinner with Governor Patten. He has been my Governor in Hong Kong for a good many years now, following his outstanding success in introducing our Community Charge to a grateful British people.

"If you'll just let me finish," I said to his wife, Mrs Patten, when she offered me a canapé before the meal. "It's never advisable to wear your hair like that. Your type of hair is much better short. Otherwise it gets in the eyes, and one can't have that."

After another glass of Scotch, I set about solving the poor woman's curtain problem.

"You don't want them overflowing at the bottom, dear," I was good enough to advise her. "That way, they gather dust. You want them cut off an inch to an inch-and-a-half above the floor. That way, the dust drops to the ground — and your dust problem is solved!!"

I dipped into my handbag for my trusty pair of kitchen scissors. I never go anywhere without them, not since 1983, when I asked Francis Pym to leave my Cabinet and the poor man proved difficult.

❖

"If one wants a job done well, one must do it oneself," I sighed. I then got down on my hands and knees and set about trimming those curtains to the proper size.

"Margaret, why not join us for dinner now?" It was my Governor, barracking me — ME! — to take my seat. It surprised me, the way forty grown men could sit around a table, eating and drinking, when there was work to be done. My goodness! That's not my way, never has been, never will be!

"If you'll just let me go on!" I said, snipping with vigour in search of real results.

"We just didn't want your dinner to get cold," he interrupted.

"One moment, please! We have a job to do! If you'll just let me finish!"

After another glass of Scotch, we had completed our task, the excess material lay vanquished, and the dust-trap was no more. Rejoice!

❖

Needless to say, the grandees continued making small talk, chewing and swallowing. That's never been my way. Did we really want to leave Hong Kong with dust on the curtains? What sort of legacy is that? Let no one ever accuse me of neglecting the details. It's not in my nature.

After another glass of Scotch, I made my way to the table, sat down on my cushioned chair, and informed the assembled company of their timetable for tomorrow.

"Margaret!" My Governor interrupted me with another hiss. "That's no cushion — that's Mr Ling, Chairman of the Allied and Corporate Bank of East Asia!"

Supported by his advice, I moved to a more dominant position. Mr Ling, who was only small, looked in no fit state to sit around anyone's table, let alone my Governor's. After another glass of Scotch, I laid aside special time to tell everyone how to tie their shoelaces correctly, with the minimum of wastage.

❖

Breakfast the next morning with my new Leader of the Opposition.

"William Hague! William Hague!" I told him. "Have you got that? Have you? William Hague! William Hague! Remember that name! William Hague!"

"Yes, that's my name. My name is William Hague," he chipped in, cockily.

"If you'll let me continue! Do have the good manners to let me go on!" I said, reasonably. "I am talking about the young man I have appointed to lead the Conservative Party. Young. Bald. Northern. I forget his name."

"William Hague!" he interrupted.

"That's it! William Hague! William Hague! Have you got it? Have you? Remember that name! William Hague!"

After another glass of Scotch, I was good enough to give him some tips on how to lead the party for me. "We must tackle it vigorously so that not a shred remains! Freedom under the rule of law! Ministers decide! Frit! Frit! Fritz? Where? Schmidt? Dreadful man! German! Not good! Remember the Good Samaritan! Remember that name! Treachery with a smile on its face! The Lady's not for turning! Rejoice! Rejoice! Have you got that? Have you? Have you?"

The young man nodded. "That's excellent advice, Lady

Thatcher' he said. "Thank you most kindly."

"If you'll just let me finish!" I sighed. Why do people insist on interrupting one so? But we women are used to it. After another glass of Scotch, I dipped into my bag, took out my scissors and set to work thinning out his lapels. The British people will never trust a man with wide lapels, and certainly not young whatsisname.

❖

In the afternoon, I generously agreed to my proposal to perform an historic walkabout. This gave the ordinary, decent people of Hong Kong the chance to congratulate me on the way I have stood up to the Chinese these past twenty years by:

a) sticking up for the absolute right of the people of Hong Kong to self-government by Peking; and

b) granting a copper-bottomed guarantee that we will ensure the basic human freedom of the ordinary, decent people of Hong Kong to remain in Hong Kong under Chinese rule, like it or not.

After another glass of Scotch, I launched myself into the bustling streets, full of cornershops and customers. Those doughty folk leapt into doorways at my approach, obviously determined to grant a figure of my world stature a clear path through their streets.

After another glass of Scotch, I darted into a Chinese restaurant. Like any ordinary housewife, I headed for the kitchen. A little man was boiling noodles.

"You don't want to do it like that!" I told him. "You want to fry noodles first, then boil! And no one eats noodles anymore — the future lies in the poached egg! Excuse me! If you'll just let me finish!"

But he refused to listen to sound British commonsense. After a quick glass of Scotch, I dipped into my handbag and got out my scissors. His neck-scarf was a positive dust-trap. A woman's work is never done.

PAUL THEROUX'S
HAPPY NEW YEAR

I remember one Christmas with particular pleasure. I was on Cape Cod with my family and a close friend, Princess Margaret, who was at that time sister to the Queen of England.

It was an extraordinary three days. On Christmas Eve, Santa Claus appeared and distributed presents to the children. He struck me then as a warm-hearted, rosy-faced fellow whose capacity for generosity seemed boundless.

On Christmas Day, while the family were all roasting chestnuts around the warm glow of the log fire, I escorted Princess Margaret outside. Noticing the unashamed convexity of her tremulous breasts, I took her again and again behind the coal shed until she squealed with pleasure and howled for more. Like any great writer, for me it's the little details that are so telling. At one point her diamond coronet wobbled slightly on her head from the thrill of it all, and for that moment she forgot she wasn't Queen.

On Boxing Day, I began to revise my opinion of Santa Claus. I started to realise that in fact he was not a nice person at all, but a cold-hearted overweight has-been with the liverish complexion of a confirmed alcoholic and no true feelings for children beyond the predatory. And what had he written? Pah! The odd carol maybe, but nothing that would last. Meanwhile, I had written anything up to fifteen travel books, thirty novels, six memoirs and twelve books of literary criticism — without even trying! No wonder that when he looked at me his eyes glowed with such unseasonal envy.

❖

In England for New Year, I had a day to spare so in the morning I took the underground train from Westminster to Sloane Square and in the afternoon I wrote a book about it.

As I boarded the train at Westminster, I noticed that everyone apart from me was squat and ugly and dishevelled and grimy. The English have never recovered from their loss of Empire, and their faces and bodies have become raddled with self-pity as a result. Among them I felt an alien: I sensed their eyes glaring at me with undeserved contempt. No one spoke a word to me as the train rattled along. Instead, they buried their heads in their newspapers, pretending to read as they plotted ways to kill me. I knew from their sullen silence that they would like me to fall beneath the wheels of the train. Only then would they smile. I had lived in England for thirty-five years, but never once had I felt any warmth.

The next stop was St James's Park. Opposite me sat a statuesque Masai woman, her body made sleek and strong by her daily hunts for wildebeest in the foothills of the

Serengetti, her voluminous breasts swaying gently in the winter breeze. I asked her whether this was the Circle Line, and before the train had set off she had placed her hunting spear to one side and was howling eagerly in the ecstasy of sex like an addict injected, and her eyes rolled up in her skull and she stared, still howling, with big white eyes like a blind zombie that sees everything. "Paul! Paul!" she cried — she must have read my name off my clutchbag — "You are not only a great writer, much better than the over-rated V.S. Naipaul, for instance — but you are *all man!!*" Afterwards, limp and sleepy, stupefied by sex, she confirmed that, yes, this was the Circle Line. As the train drew into Westminster, she rose to leave.

I never saw her again. I now realise that I never really liked her anyway and I bet she couldn't get a piece into the New Yorker even if she really tried.

❖

Few readers realise that no one has ever attempted a paragraph exactly like this in the whole history of English literature. Dickens and Hardy both wrote paragraphs, yes, but they didn't contain exactly these words. Ditto James, Fielding, Melville, Waugh, Fitzgerald, Borges and even Shakespeare. They might have aimed for it, but their time and their talent was against them. Naipaul? Nowhere near. So what I am doing in this paragraph — starting with the word "Few", then going on for precisely 101 words, ending with the word "Enjoy" — is utterly unique in the annals of letters, comparable in brilliance only with itself. *Enjoy.*

❖

The duty of every artist is to the truth, and to the truth alone. That is what separates him from the rest of mankind, who fill their days with half-truths, evasions, fibs and lies. I learnt the importance of truth on New Year's Day over half a lifetime ago. I was travelling to the peak of Everest with

Sir Edmund Hillary and Sherpa Tensing. As I was pulling the two of them up the last few feet, I surveyed the mountain-tops below me, all swathed in cloud. "I am now on top of the world" I thought. "Truth is my only friend."

At that point, the English aristocrat Lady Antonia Fraser appeared beside me in a straw hat carrying a picnic basket. She was wearing a shimmering cotton dress of floral design, the top four buttons open to the bracing air, exposing the upper swell of her bountiful breasts.

Looking down, I checked that Sir Edmund and Sherpa Tensing were still struggling uphill on their ice-skates. They would be a good few minutes yet. I congratulated Lady Antonia on her "Mary Queen of Scots" and with a flicker of her eyelashes she congratulated me for being much, much more intelligent than V.S. Naipaul. Then Lady Antonia removed all her clothes, placed her straw hat neatly on the picnic-basket and lay writhing in the warm embrace of the gently yielding snow screaming "Take me! Take me, you great big hunk of a tormented yet strangely accessible and darkly comic American writer, you!" There was something in her posture that aroused me. During sex, she squeaked with pleasure like a field mouse, scampering this way and that, her legs a-quiver, her nose twitching in ecstasy. When it was over, she beseeched me for more, but I told her I had to give a hand to Hillary and Tensing. Looking down at them, I noticed their eyes were filled with ill-disguised resentment at me for having reached the top first, and then having taken Lady Antonia. I knew then that, like everyone else in the world, they would never acknowledge my achievements. Some people are so self-absorbed they just can't face up to the truth — but that's human beings for you.

EMMA THOMPSON'S
SENSE AND SENSIBILITY DIARY

Thursday 6 April: Jemima arrives on set, very energised. She has a bit of an itch on her left shoulder for a few seconds, but simply refuses to make a song and dance about it, just carrying on as if nothing had happened. How I admire her. She's the bravest of the brave, that girl.

Friday 7 April: Hotel quite nice. Make note to put this observation as "local colour" in my Diary.

Saturday 8 April: Tenser than fuck. Fucker than tense. Done in and utterly frazzled. It's as hard as buggery willing oneself into the language and thought of Austen's England. First day nerves, I suppose. Ha. If only I were more like my wretched "luvvie" image. But I'm too fucking down-to-earth, that's the pissing-off thing. That's the trouble with being an actor: you're like a soldier in the trenches on the Western Front, alone but for a single red rose, utterly naked as the rain pisses down and the enemy brush their hair and put on their make-up, all ready for another day of heavy fucking shelling.

Sunday 9 April: Robert (Hardy) tells us he's just found the most marvellous little old lady in the street, utterly entrancing and delightful. "A little bit of olde England that shalt always been mine owneth, methinks" he says. Robert's speech has the natural nuance and fluidity of the 19th century. Send note to production manager: would it be poss. to locate little old lady and wrap her up for Robert as end-of-shoot leaving pressie? Says he'll see what he can do.

Monday 10 April: Director Ang takes us through our meditation and exercises. We sit on cushions and breathe deeply, imagining ourselves to be fallen leaves, slowly disintegrating into the deep brown rich English ground beneath us. Sadly, Fred, the assistant studio manager is not informed of this, arriving with a broom and attempting to sweep us up. Eating a pear, I think to myself that on occasion, humans can be prone to muddle. I fancy Jane might have rather approved of this observation.

Thursday 13 April: Wake up in middle of night. Bit weepy. Try to picture myself as Bosnian refugee, starving from lack of food. Imagine the hunger. Tearful. Suddenly feel peckish, wolf down a Mars Bar. Feel dreadfully guilty — much guiltier than John Major and his philistine cohorts have ever managed to feel!

Friday 14 April: Spot on chin. Fuckity fuck. Hate Mars Bars to buggery. Stressed. Bit weepy. Light anti-stress candle in bathroom. Have a pee. Misfire and put out candle. Fuck. Sob.

Monday 24 April: Long psychological investigations of characters over dinner. Alan says Elinor is basically a control freak, pass carrots please. I say she's the kind of woman who's always looking for a centre of gravity and could probably do with a bloody good shag, have you finished with the sprouts down that end when you're quite ready. Ang nods. I think he is surprised by the depth of thought English actors put into it all, and how we wrestle so deeply with our characters. Delving into his own character, Robert Hardy says Sir John Middleton is every bit the old-fashioned English country gent with the slightly theatrical delivery, but with a shorter wig than usual, which he appreciates, as it avoids what Jane would no doubt have called the itchy-ear syndrome.

Wednesday 26 April: A thrilling English morn 'midst the ravishing English countryside. In break from shoot, I take a stroll. Sunken roads are beautiful to behold and Devon lambs remarkably handsome. On Dartmoor, I meet a small boy.

Me: Hello.

Boy: H'llo.

Me: This is a thrilling English morn 'midst the ravishing English countryside.

Boy: Come again?

Me: I said, this is a thrilling English morn 'midst the ravishing English countryside.

Boy: Tch. Huh. Ugh. Yuk.

Me: Country people with their earthy monosyllables and fruitful apostrophes are so much more real than the media crowd. How I yearn for such a sense of instinctive reality in my giddy, hectic life!

Boy: *Go feck yer'sel'.*

Pure Jane! I laugh my most natural laugh. Ah, England!

Friday 5 May: Hugh Grant all over newspapers for having it off with an LA prostitute. Feel dreadfully sorry for Hugh, getting all this rotten publicity. How I loathe the Murdoch papers. How can they publish this ghastly stuff, when it's none of their business? Let's hope it all dies down and is forgotten over the next few months. Remind myself to put Hugh/prostitute incident in my diary of the film shoot in time for publication mid-Feb.

Monday 7 May: New hotel quite nice. Jot it down.

Thursday 11 May: On lavvy with bowel probs. Start to hate myself. Omigod. Grow a little weepy. Thank fuck I have a fully developed sense of humour. Thank you, Monty Python, Jane Austen and a hundred other influences. At least I have learned to laugh at myself. But now is neither the time nor the place for jokes — I just don't see what's so funny, that's all — so I decide not to. Why the fuck should I? Eh? Instead, I light a joss stick, massage my pressure points and look caringly into the mirror. Spot back on chin.

Tuesday 16 May: I have just ovulated, so I draw the company together. "I've just ovulated" I announce, with unnerving honesty. I sense they love me for it, so inevitably I grow a bit sobby, "So let's be very, very quiet for three minutes" I continue, "and **think** our way into being an egg". Alan Rickman goes on for longer than anyone else, at least six minutes. In my opinion, he gives a marvellously **hard-boiled** performance, bless him.

GORE VIDAL

A
S I once said to the late Jack Kennedy, brushing my hand with due caution yet infinite tenderness against his inner thigh: "The publishing industry must take the blame for all these wretched books". Ambulate elegantly into a public library, accepting with a dignified flourish of the well-manicured hand the applause of passers-by, and what is it that confronts one? Books, books, and yet more books.

James Joyce, archbore Irishman; Jane Austen, beskirted miniaturist; Henry James, pot-bellied obscurantist; William Wordsworth, grubby-fingered horticulturalist; George Eliot, flat-chested moraliser; William Shakespeare, AC/DC Midlands thespian: it saddens me to say I have never managed to wade to the end of any of their no doubt immensely — one might venture to say *grindingly* — distinguished works.

The continued publication of these dogged dullards raises fascinating questions about the publishing "industry", as it chooses to term itself. Contrast the massed sales of these authors the world over with the pitiful circulation of my own, somewhat more sparky output. Gore Vidal sells poorly in Germany, Austria, Spain, Portugal and Scandinavia, precious little in Greece, Turkey and points east. And for the past few years the citizens of Yugoslavia have been forced to undergo the pain of finding *no Vidal whatsoever* in their bookshops. Small wonder they look so horribly — as Wallis Windsor might have put it — boo-hooey.

❖

But there is, as I found cause to remark in characteristically aphoristic mood to the feminine but nonetheless quirkily attractive Eleanor Roosevelt, a reason for everything.

So what, one might ask, is the reason behind the universal conspiracy against sales of my collected works? I know from a long-time associate of Henry Kissinger that it is to be located deep in the heart of the CIA, in union with the all-powerful Firearms Lobby of the USA and the combined might of the war-machine, the Mafia, the Pentagon and a top secret anti-Vidal committee of the United Nations, headed by the notoriously slack-buttocked Deng Xiaoping.

Money, that most omnivorous of commodities, is in charge once more: by diverting the fortune that would otherwise have been spent on my novels, essays and memoirs straight into the international war machine, the governments of the world hope to coax their citizens into paranoia and xenophobia, and thus to support them in their battle for re-election. Informed accounts suggest the innocent Mr Lee Harvey Oswald had entered the Dallas Book Pound that fateful day simply to borrow my recently-published "Julian"; and look what happened to him.

❖

My antecedents, seasoned aristocrats all, were the founders of what we are now pleased to describe, in our impishly ironic way, as The Land of the Free and the Home of the Brave. My great-grandfather, Senator Bore Vidal of New York, the owner of two hundred thousand acres of prime farming land east of Buffalo, married my great-grandmother Edwina Crashing, the daughter of Amelia Crashing, whose father was one of the Wilds of Montana, giving birth to my grandfather, Senator Wild Crashing Bore, who in turn married Miss Gore Blimey from one of the most influential aristocratic families in London's gorgeously affluent Hackney East. From their union sprang, with, I regret to say, more promptitude than pulchritude, the Hon. Mrs Bore V. Dull of Oklahoma, who then gave birth to a famously talented son, Gore V. Dull, later to become better known as Gore Vidal, now widely respected as the nation's foremost novelist, social commentator and historian.

On my father's side, I am related to Abraham Lincoln and Thomas Jefferson, neither of them inconsiderable figures in the political arena, though one must learn, I suppose, to overlook their deficiencies in the facial hair department. On the military side, my distinguished great-great-grandfather General Gore L. Vidal was at Custer's side at The Battle of Little Big Horn. Many believe it to have been General Gore's personal message of encouragement to the troops ("TO THE FIRST MAN WHO GETS OUT OF HERE ALIVE, A FREE SHAMPOO AND SET") that swung the balance in that least dainty of skirmishes. In turn, General Gore's great-nephew, Sassoon Vidal, the founder of the first literary salon, emerged as the major poet of the 1st World War, no anthology complete without his moving lines: "The shells burst all about us/Spraying mud o'er our uniforms/Clean on this bleak morn".

My English critics have attempted to ignore the illustrious

and influential pedigree from which I so deftly sprang. But then no-one of any breeding cares any more about that inconsiderable little offshore isle, sinking beneath the weight of its own — how shall I put it? — snobbery.

❖

It requires no uncanny knowledge of the human heart to figure out that the Christian "religion", if one can still call it that, has had, as it were, its day.

From the unhygienic Joseph through the ill-assorted fish-filleters, so many of them called Simon or Andrew, right the way through to those dreary and unseasonably bewooled baa-lambs for whom the Good Lord reserved such an inexplicably soft spot in his squeaky-clean heart, the assorted personages in the New Testament make for unattractive companions.

As I indicated as early as 1951 to my old friend, the over-promoted Jack Kennedy, Christianity is a past-time that is most unlikely ever to catch on. At that point, incidentally, Jack turned to me, chuckled, "Gore, you are this nation's one true genius", gave me the most delicate peck on my cheek, and turned back to the job in hand, which necessarily involved a youthful representative of the female community, complete with the obligatory appendages and protrusions of her species.

How much more sensible, I would venture, to found a religion upon someone altogether more worthy of adoration. My own faith requires little more than a mirror, a blow-drier and the merest touch of Estee Lauder navy-blue eye-liner. I worship three or four times a day, for up to five hours at a time. The object of my worship has never let me down, growing ever more divine with each kiss blown, gently salivating in the reciprocation of our mutual esteem. Toujours l'amour; toujours Gore.

PETER YORK

Did you have a *wonderful* time? *Did* you have a wonderful time? Did you? Was it a wonderful time that you had? In the Eighties, I mean. The Eighties. And all *that stuff*.

A *strange* business, the Eighties. They were really more than a decade, of course. They were a *lifestyle option*. Ten years when we all read World of Interiors in our Designer Conservatories as we sipped Conran's Extra Virgin Olive Oil while listening to Duran Duran while ordering our BT shares on our cordless phones.

Peter York: Arthur, in the Eighties, what was your own particular favourite Extra Virgin Olive Oil?

Arthur Scargill: I didn't have one.

Peter York: Of course, we're talking pre-*Carluccio's Own Label*, here, aren't we? And to what extent were Spandau

Ballet an influence on you during the early Eighties?

Arthur Scargill: We didn't have the time for that. My lads were *striking*.

Peter York: *Very* striking. All that *designer grime*. In the early Eighties, the British Miners were right up there with *Depeche Mode* and even *Sham 69*. And the Miners Strike became one of the most exciting lifestyle options of the Eighties, the perfect real-life Theme Park accompaniment to "Do You Really Want To Hurt Me?" by the *desperately* important Boy George.

❖

But if one chap can be said to have invented the Eighties, and *moulded* (a very Eighties concept, that) Government Economic Policy and a full *ratatouille* of social reforms, then that chap was surely Marilyn. Marilyn began the Eighties as a transvestite hat-checker at the infinitely profound Blitz club, and ended it as senior policy adviser to Mrs Thatcher herself, *unofficial*, if you will, and rarely, *if ever*, in direct contact with the Divine Mrs T herself, but unsurpassingly *influential* nonetheless.

Peter York: Marilyn, how were the Eighties for you?

Marilyn: Well, the Eighties were all about looking good. It was show-business. By which I mean not just business, but *show* and *business*, and if you put the two together, that's *show* and *business*, then what you end up with is show *plus* business, which equals *business-show*. Yeah, that's it. And it made us all feel very deep. Like, at very least four foot deep, maybe five.

Peter York: And as early as 1982, you were the unseen hand behind the far-reaching reforms initiated by the Social Affairs Unit...

Marilyn: Come again?

❖

In what way did the Eighties differ from the Seventies? What way, *José*? For a surprisingly large number of us, The

Seventies came before the Eighties, in a Bay-City-Rollerish sort of way. In the Seventies, we were drinking *Lucozade* — a very *fizzy-drinkish* thing to do — and in the Eighties we were drinking Capuccino, all *frothy* and *chocolatey* and *YOU-magaziney*. In the Seventies, we were all rummaging around stray dustbins — and horribly *dustbinny* they were too — in the hope of finding a half-eaten sandwich or a stray rat to chew on. But as the Eighties gathered steam, we found we had forgotten about the dustbins and we were dining out at *Le Manoir aux Quat' Saisons* (very *French*, very *restauranty*, very *Eighties*), probably with our very own *style consultant*.

❖

One fellow more than any other was responsible for the way we lived and breathed in the Eighties. But we couldn't get him to give us an interview, or anyone else for that matter, so we settled for Alfred Sherman (very *Alfred*, very *Sherman*), widely seen by *those in the know* (and the Eighties was all about those in the know — remember?) as a *fat and distinctly disagreeable* self-publicist who'd never turn down an opportunity to exaggerate his own importance to those gullible enough to go along with it.

Alfred Sherman: I invented Thatcherism. I single-handedly transformed the British economy. I was the First Man on the Moon. And I tell you this: I'll never forgive that Neil Armstrong for taking the credit.

Peter York: What does Spandau Ballet mean to you?

Alfred Sherman: Gary Kemp this, Gary Kemp that. But I was the one who wrote the songs, and they never even credited me with playing bass on their first three albums. But historians will see that the bass-line on those first three albums by the Spandaus was the prime influence on Margaret Thatcher when she came to send a Task Force to the Falklands.

Peter York: And finally, by the end of the Eighties, you had become disillusioned by the progress the Tories had made?

Alfred Sherman: I had given Margaret everything — the loan of my rooms at Number 10 Downing Street, complete freedom to follow my instructions and the prestige attached to an association with me. And how had she repaid me? Not a single mention of me in her autobiography. Not one! And to think that I had been the one who had pulled the strings to get her into the House of Lords...

❖

There was an *awful* lot of shopping in the Eighties. When we went into shops, we'd often take out our money from our Armani wallets then buy something — *and take it away with us*. Food shopping in particular was *very* voguey. And *after* you had bought the food and taken it home — *you would sure as hell want to eat the stuff*. The world was divided into those who ate it by themselves and those who ate in the company of others, brought in to supplement their *lifestyle*. In many ways, food taught us how to *re-invent* ourselves. But it left us feeling confused. And a *teensy bit guilty*. This was the boil-in-the-bag, very *Next*, pre-Major culture of the post-Bowie era, with perhaps a dab of *Neighbours*, and what it said was this: "There's an awful lot of *stuff* around, and we've got a *momentum* going, so let's *run with it* and — fingers crossed — soon the stuff with the momentum will *get stuffed*!" So being someone who bought food from shops in the Eighties and then ate it *became one* of those terribly defining things. You lucky people!

❖

The Eighties were, in the end, quintessentially and characteristically very, very, very *Eighties*. Without *them*, the Nineties would have followed straight on from the Seventies — and there would have been a world *without Spandau Ballet*. But if the Eighties taught us anything, they taught us that *a little goes a long way* and — let's never forget it, boys and girls — *italicisation sells*.

YOU AND YOURS

Mark Whittaker: Sit back and enjoy the ride — or can you?! — because today on You and Yours we ask whether the government's repeated failure to provide compulsory safety-belts on playground swings is responsible for the deaths of up to several children a year —

Liz Barclay: And we ask why aren't petrol pumps in the nation's major filling stations clearly marked with a "Do Not Drink" sign? We tackle the government minister in question and ask him whether he would be prepared to drink a litre of premium grade petrol in the studio and face the consequences.

Mark Whittaker: Also on You and Yours, the red paint that can cause you great distress if you spread it all over your tongue — and the state-registered GP who claims he has no regrets about informing a single mother on benefit that a front door left wide open can lead to severe household draughts.

Liz Barclay: All this plus a fair deal for the vegetarian butcher's assistant who has been threatened with the sack if he refuses to sell meat — in today's You and Yours.

Mark Whittaker: But first on today's programme, it's been over five hundred years since the Black Death wrought havoc on ordinary households the length and breadth of the country. But over the past few weeks there have been distressing signs that another deadly virus is set to strike. With me in the studio is Professor R.T. Fishial, a leading expert in the field of contrived health scares. Professor Fishial, what are the tell-tale signs that Britain is set to be wiped out by a bogus virus every bit as terrible as the Black Death — and is there anything we can do about it?

Professor R.T. Fishial: The signs cannot be ignored. Already I've heard people talk of a major international bogus catastrophe, perhaps even on the scale of last year's widespread terror that fresh food causes cancer.

Mark Whittaker: And is there anything the ordinary man or woman on the street can do to prevent themselves dying a hideous death within the next few hours?

Professor R.T. Fishial: Nothing whatever.

Mark Whittaker: Great! Thanks!

Professor R.T. Fishial: That'll be seventy-five pounds plus VAT, please.

Liz Barclay: And now to a matter of growing concern among regular users of hats, caps and assorted headwear. Mrs E. White from Esher in Surrey has e-mailed us to say that the beret-style hat she purchased at her local branch of Dorothy Perkins last April proved wholly unsuitable for the job for which she bought it, namely as a miniature kitchen-sink. "The beret is made of a light fabric which simply does not hold water," Mrs White tells us. "After thirty separate washing-up sessions, my kitchen floor was utterly soaked — and the beret itself was ruined." Well, we tracked down the manager of that particular branch of Dorothy Perkins and we have him on the line now. Mr Avery, I must put it to you that you have completely ruined Mrs White's life. What do you propose to do about giving her a fair deal?

Mr Avery: Well, to be honest the beret was never really intended for use as a sink...

Liz Barclay: And were warnings to that effect clearly labelled on it at the time of purchase?

Mr Avery: Well, er —

Liz Barclay: Thank you, Mr Avery. We now go over to the Liberal Democrat spokesman with special responsibility for supporting consumer complaints on daytime radio, Roger Jessop. If I may turn to you, Mr Jessop —

Roger Jessop MP: Frankly, Liz, I'm deeply distressed by what we have just heard. I'll be seeking immediate cross-party talks in the House of Commons with a view to setting up a tribunal to look into the whole matter of setting up a Beretwatch actionline to deal with the whole problem of porous berets and I'll also be contacting the Office of Fair Trading to look into the whole matter of how to look into the whole matter.

Mark Whittaker: But for the time being, you can e-mail us on whingers dot uk dot crybaby dot BBC stress dot timewaster dot. And now to more of your calls on faulty bus signing. Mr Mark Ryland of Aldershot tells us that he caught a bus from Newhaven wanting to go to Eastbourne but he ended up in Reading High Street. The bus company claims that the bus was clearly marked "Reading", but Mr Ryland — whose dog Scruff died just two years ago, and who himself suffers from occasional vertigo — tells us that he took this to mean that passengers were permitted to carry books and/or magazines with them. Mr Ryland, whose wife left him last May and whose cousin recently broke his leg in a skiing accident, has since called on Reading Council to urgently consider changing the name of the town, but he has met what he describes as a very negative response. Liz?

Liz Barclay: And on tomorrow's You and Yours, we call for tighter controls on everything that doesn't have them already, we hear tell of the potentially lethal threat to the gardener from brightly coloured flowers, and we investigate complaints against the complaints commissioner and ask him whether there should be a commissioner appointed to look into them, and if so how one would set about complaining about him — all this, and a major investigation into the man who has been refused a job as an air traffic controller for no better reason than because he is blind.

YULETIDE WITH
NOEL EDMONDS

There's been a right old merry ding-dong on high! *Stop it, it's hurting*!!! You've gotta giggle, haven't you? 'Cos let's face it, Christmas — hey "Chris", where's the "mouse"?? (forgive the terrible pun!!) — all comes down to telly.

There's morning telly in the bedroom, for when you're unwrapping the old stockings. There's lunchtime telly, for when you're all scoffing the old turkey and trimmings round the kitchen gogglebox. And then there's afternoon and evening telly — for when Dad's dozing off in the corner, the lovely young Fiona is half-naked upstairs snoggin' the bloke next door, and Mum's up to her knees in brandy butter and wrapping paper!! And if you want a "telly good Christmas", as the little Jap bloke might put it, then you need look no further than the special Yuletide edition of *Noel's Christmas Telly Addicts*, coming shortly to a small screen near you.

I'll be asking some very searching questions about the real message behind the historical Christmas. Among the questions I'll be asking the Walton family from Droitwich and the Kemble family from Warrington are: Who got the sprig of holly caught in her bloomers in the 1973 Xmas edition of *On The Buses*? And what was the name of the actor who played Santa in 1981 *Only Fools and Horses Xmas Special*? Ah, Christmas: as the late lamented Jesus almost said, it's a time for light entertainment for all mankind.

❖

On a more serious note, a number of people I greatly respect in this industry have turned round to me and said, "You're a marvellous *broadcaster*, Noel, a true *professional* with your trademark beard and *talent for communication* and you've made Christmas your *very own*." To which I turn round and say, "Thanks, fellas — and I'm happy to say that one of my wholly-owned Noel subsidiary companies now owns 100% European broadcast transmission rights to Christmas. We're not talking just Santa Claus here but Jesus Christ and his entire family including crib, innkeeper and livestock. I'm proud to say they're all now the property of 'First No-el plc'." At the moment they're in development for what will prove a very exciting and creative multi-media branded commercial format for a prime-time slot.

Joseph, for instance. In broadcasting terms — and let's face it, we're in the communication game — Joseph is a woefully under-developed character. So let's all turn round and say it, loud and clear: the guy's a weak link. But get in a first-rate gag-writer and a highly professional producer, add a bit, take away a bit, chivvy him up a bit, and your Josephs could be up there with your Cillas and your Beadles. We're after the truly masterly David Jason to play Joseph in the Official Crinkly Bottom Nativi-panto this year, with Pauline Quirke as Mary and Dipsy and La-la from the fabulous Teletubbies — you can't argue with figures — as the farm animals! Great entertainment, very Xmasy, very Noel Edmonds. And — who knows? — we might find ourselves up to a few of our old tricks with a ton of gunge to be unceremoniously dumped on a Wise Man not a million miles from the lovely Patrick Moore — but my lips are sealed! Ooh — you've got me going again! Tee-hee! At this point, I turn into the proverbial giggle-machine!!!

❖

I don't mean this unkindly, but I do find it fascinating to look back on those colleagues I was with in the early days of Radio One and see what's happened to them all now. Tony Blackburn. Alan Freeman. Pete Murray. Ed Stewart. The word forgotten springs to mind. Believe me, I have the greatest sympathy for them. In those days, I only had the mid-morning weekend slot, and these were broadcasters I looked up to. Now I want to take them to one side, pin back their old lug 'oles and turn around and ask them, "Why did it go down the pan, mate? Where did it all go pear-shaped?" But I'll always try to help them if I can. I've already arranged a booking on the House Party for Tony Blackburn in early March. He's agreed to be tarred and feathered by ordinary members of the public and then thrown naked — except for his toupee! — into a vat of fast-drying red paint! Should be a lot of fun. If you count yourself a professional in this business, you've got to stick by your old mates through thick and thin — or thick and fat, in Ed's case. Sorry, Ed — only kidding!! That's not a dig at Ed, by the way. I just feel sorry for the guy.

❖

Of course, Christmas is traditionally a time for some truly memorable practical jokes from yours truly, the King of the Wind-Up Merchants! Without giving the game away, I've gotta tell you that this Yule we've got some great thoroughly seasonal practical gags we're specially going to perform on you, the ordinary viewing public.

❖

GAG 1: We secretly remove the "DANGER — THIN ICE" from a picture-postcard lake! Then we sit back and watch while the Ormerod family of Chesterfield — Sue, 45, builder Gary, 46, Auntie June, 44, and — one for all you gentlemen in the audience! — lovely teenage daughter Meg, 15 — strap on their skates, march straight into the middle, fall through the ice — *and sink*!!!!! With famous well-known celebrity Barry Ross of TV's *Casualty*, we then spring a Noel-style surprise on Gary, 46, as he languishes in Intensive Care! Dressed in surgeons' uniforms, we enter the ward, pull off our masks — and sing "Freeze a Jolly Good Fellow!", waving the tell-tale sign above our heads. Gotcha, Gary!

❖

GAG 2: Blobby, blobby, blobby! Your friend and mine surprises Jack Hasker, 25, an ordinary member of the viewing public as he sits watching telly in his Y-fronts! Mr Blobby then throws poor old Jack into a bath which we have previously filled with — wait for it! — *dead toads*!!! We then require him to *swallow them* — cheered on by TV celebrity Carol Vorderman! But believe me, Jack — we only do it to people we like!

❖

Blobby-blobby-blobby!!! Tune in on Xmas Day and you'll see him in his most legendary role yet — *Away In A Manger*, starring the Blobby Jesus!!! Love it! "Joyeux No-el"!